C000144792

The Gleam of the Lines

...te evening train, Kildare, December 2009 (2c/Hugh Dempsey)

The original Boyne Viaduct at Drogheda, painted by Roger Curzon in 1878 (Drogheda Municipal Art Collection, Highlanes Gallery).

R. Curzon

Dublin, Wicklow and Wexford Railway 2–4–0 No. 14 at
Woodenbridge Junction, *c.*1890, a painting by Norman Whitla.

IE railcar travelling at speed through the countryside of Co. Kildare, June 2009 (2c/Hugh Dempsey).

The Gleam of the Lines

An illustrated journey through two centuries of Irish railway history

TOM FERRIS

MR/NCC A Class 4–4–0 No. 65, hauling the 'Holden Train', built for Larne businessman A.W. Holden in 1903 (F. Moore) (above).
Midland Great Western Grendon 2–4–0 No. 2 at Broadstone Shed, Dublin, 1865, in a painting by Norman Whitla (left).

To Elizabeth, for putting up with my obsession and pointing me in the direction of the title.

Published in Ireland by
Gill & Macmillan
Hume Avenue, Park West, Dublin 12
with associated companies throughout the world

www.gillmacmillan.ie

Text © Tom Ferris 2011

ISBN 978 0 7171 5002 1

Concept and design © Bookcraft Ltd 2011
www.bookcraft.co.uk

Project managed by John Button
Designed by Lucy Guenot

Set in 12 on 15 point Minion.

Endpaper images:
Front: Midland Great Western Railway D Class 4–4–0 No. 2 *Jupiter* near Mallaranny, 1895, painted by Norman Whitla.
Back: IE express speeding under Pike's Bridge, Co. Kildare (Bart Busschots).

All rights reserved.

No part of this publication may be copied, reproduced or transmitted in any form or by any means, without the
written permission of the publishers.

All images included in this volume are in the public domain, with the exception of those credited in individual captions.
Many of the images come from books, brochures, maps and postcards forming part of Bookcraft Ltd's 'Times Past Archive'
(see www.memoriesoftimespast.com)

Every effort has been made to ensure the accuracy of the information presented in this book, and every reasonable effort
has been made to trace copyright holders.
The publishers will not assume liability for damages caused by inaccuracies in the data, or for any copyright inadvertently breached,
and make no warranty whatsoever expressed or implied.
The publishers welcome comments and corrections from readers, which will be incorporated in future editions.

A CIP catalogue record for this book is available from the British Library.

5   4   3   2   1

Printed in Malaysia for Imago

CONTENTS

Castlebar station, Co. Mayo,
April 1989 (Felix Ormerod).

Robert Stephenson's *Mercury*, 1830, one of the first successful steam locomotives to run on rails, from J.G. Pangborn's 1894 book *The World's Rail Way: Historical, Descriptive, Illustrative.*

It took a little longer before the first rumblings of this seismological shift were felt in Ireland. The idea of building a railway to link Dublin with its new harbour at Kingstown first emerged in a bill presented to parliament in 1825. The sandbanks and shallow waters of Dublin Bay had always made entry to the port hazardous, and by 1800 ships of more than 200 tons could not safely enter. An Act of 1815 created a Board of Commissioners for an Asylum Harbour, a refuge for ships waiting to go up the Liffey. Its location was to be the hitherto sleepy village of Dunleary, where the sands of Dublin Bay gave way to much deeper waters. To mark the use of the harbour by George IV in 1821, Dunleary was renamed Kingstown.

As Kingstown was some miles distant from Dublin, attention was now turned to providing a link from there to the city. One option favoured was a ship canal, Captain Bligh of HMS *Bounty* fame being one of its advocates. However, the growing number of apparently successful railroads across the Irish Sea pointed to a railway as an attractive alternative to the ship canal. A bill for such a railway was rejected by parliament in 1825, the year the S&D opened in England, but the following year the first Act of Parliament authorising the construction of a railway in Ireland did receive royal assent.

This was the Limerick and Waterford Railway, which was to run from Limerick via Cahir and Clonmel to Carrick-on-Suir, where it would divide, with one branch serving Waterford, another heading north to Thurles, and a third serving the coalfields in County Tipperary near Killenaule and Ballingarry. The cost of the scheme was to be £350,000. Despite the Board of Public Works offering a loan, and surveys conducted by none other than George Stephenson himself, the money could not be found to build the line. Not a single yard of track was laid, and plans for a railway from Waterford to Limerick went into limbo for close to twenty years.

The problems with the port of Dublin and access to the new harbour at Kingstown had still not been resolved by the start of the next decade, so the project to build a 'railroad' was revived (at this time 'railroad' was the usual term in both Britain and Ireland, though by the 1840s it had been largely supplanted by the word 'railway', leaving the earlier form to our American cousins). In February 1831 a provisional committee was formed to further the scheme and present a bill to Parliament. Things moved quickly and smoothly this time, and on 6 September 1831 the Act authorising the construction of the Dublin and Kingstown Railway received royal assent. The railway age in Ireland was about to begin.

The route of the Dublin and Kingstown Railway, Ireland's first passenger railway, which opened in 1834.

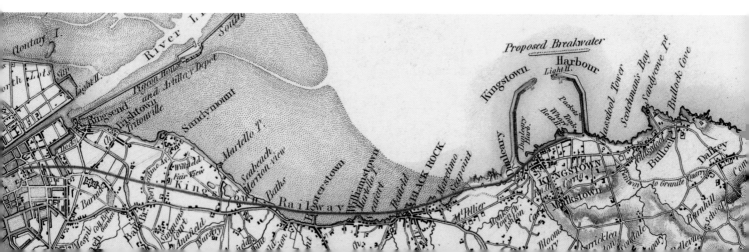

Chapter 1

BEFORE THE RAILWAYS

Before we start our exploration of the railway age in Ireland, it is worth pausing to survey the country and its transport network just before the coming of the iron road. The history of Ireland in the nineteenth century is fractured in almost every respect by the Great Famine and its aftermath. However, the first attempts to bring railways to Ireland occurred in the 1820s and 30s, in a very different country to that which came out of the Famine.

One of the most vivid pictures of pre-Famine Ireland is to be found in the *Report and Atlas of the Commissioners for Irish Railways*, sometimes referred to as the 'Drummond Commission' after Thomas Drummond, the enlightened Under-Secretary of State for Ireland, who was instrumental in the commission's appointment. This document is a valuable source of information not just to anyone with an interest in Irish railways, but in Irish history in general. It gives a remarkably vivid picture of economic conditions in the country on the eve of the Great Famine, a world that was soon to be swept away in the aftermath of the widespread potato blight which affected much of Europe in the 1840s.

A Bianconi coach leaves Dublin in the 1840s, detail of a coloured engraving by John Harris after a picture by Michaelangelo Hayes (Thomas Ross Collection).

Though it makes for a rather uninteresting mealtimes, it is possible to live on a diet consisting almost entirely of potatoes. The widespread cultivation of the crop in Ireland from the early eighteenth century onwards was a key factor in the huge growth of the population over the next hundred years. A small plot of land could produce enough potatoes to feed a whole family, so life expectancy and the size of families increased rapidly. The scions of that family could usually find enough scraps of land on which to raise their own families, and the population in many areas grew exponentially. There are few reliable statistics before the 1841 census, but at that date the population of Ireland was over 7 million.

It is against the background of this now lost world of tiny landholdings, and the decline of indigenous industries such as weaving, that the Railway Commissioners based their recommendations for a national network for the country. In the period in which the first plans for railways were being laid, contrary to often-expressed opinion, Ireland was far from being a disaster waiting to happen.

Thomas Malthus, the British writer on politics and economics best known for his theories on the dangers inherent in the growth of populations, wrote in his 1798 *Essay on the Principle of Population* that 'the

power of population is indefinitely greater than the power in the earth to produce subsistence for man.' Pre-Famine Ireland certainly reflected 'the power of population', but was it inevitable that Malthus's opinion that sooner or later an engorged population will be checked by famine and disease which would bring the country to its knees?

Most people in pre-Famine Ireland were very poor, and dangerously over-dependent on a single food source. In 1841 four-fifths of the population were rural dwellers, and 40 per cent of Irish houses were one-room mud cabins. Over seven hundred places classed as 'towns' in the 1841 census had populations of less than five hundred inhabitants.

Dublin was by far Ireland's largest city with 232,726 citizens, followed by Cork with 80,720, but Belfast was catching up rapidly with a population of 75,308. In 1844 Friedrich Engels described Dublin as a city 'possessing great attributes; however, the poorer districts are among the most hideous and repulsive to be seen in the world'. Stately Georgian squares were to be found a short stonesthrow from the squalor of the tightly-packed houses of the Liberties.

'Skibbereen' by Cork artist James Mahony, *Illustrated London News*, 1847, a stark image of the horrors of the Great Famine.

There were sporadic food shortages caused by poor harvests in 1800, 1816, 1822 and 1831, but these resulted in limited mortality. Those in 1822 and 1831 were largely confined to Connaught. There were few deaths from hunger in 1845, the first year of the potato blight, and had the disease not struck again in subsequent years the pattern of those earlier famines might have been repeated. Relief for those affected by these shortages often took the form of public works such as the building of roads. An often-overlooked feature of pre-Famine Ireland was the extent and quality of its road network. Both the county Grand Juries and the Board of Works, which was established in 1831, invested heavily in road construction and maintenance.

The Irish Railway Commissioners (see pages 33–34) carried out what today would be called a traffic census in many parts of the country, to determine whether there was likely to be enough commercial activity to support railways in those districts. Their report records high levels of traffic on the roads in many parts of the country. In Ulster's Lagan Valley road vehicles competed successfully for traffic with the canal, and

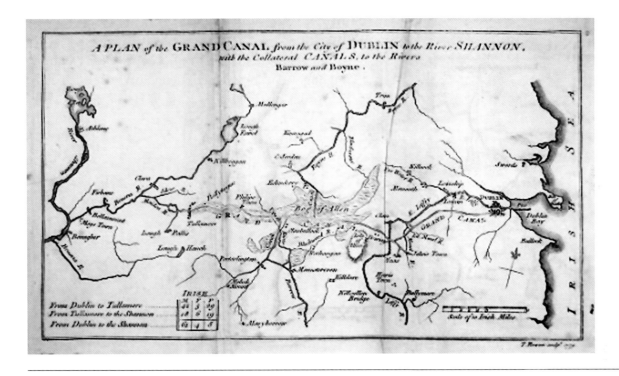

A 1779 map of the Grand Canal (above).

In the 1830s and 40s much Irish goods traffic travelled by sea and by canal: 1840 engravings of James Gandon's magnificent Custom House, the jewel in the crown of Georgian Dublin (top left); Cork Harbour (bottom left); the Royal Canal at Longford (below left); loading Grand Canal barges at the Liffey Wharf in Dublin, mid-1890s (below right).

The goods traffic map from the 1838 *Report and Atlas* (Martin Bott Collection).

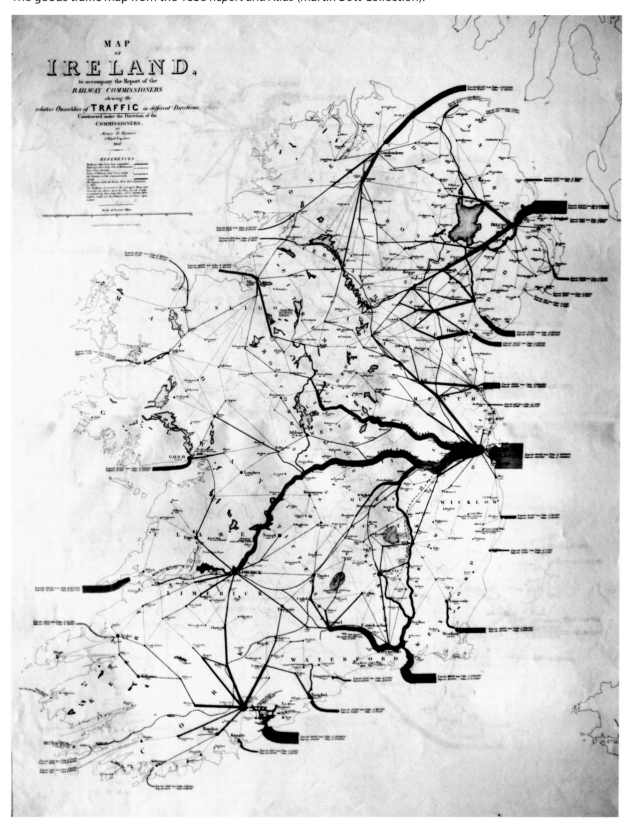

The passenger traffic map from the 1838 *Report and Atlas* (Martin Bott Collection).

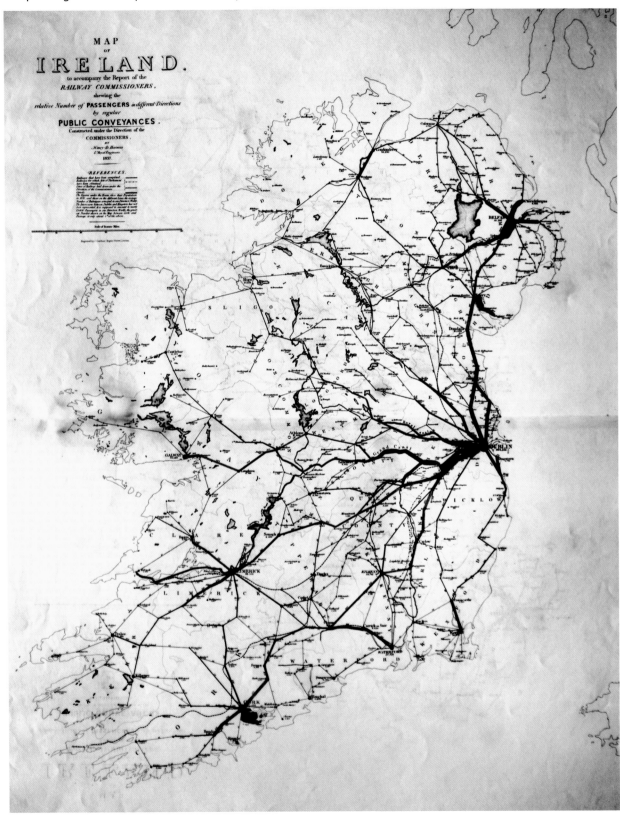

Charles Bianconi, from the frontispiece of the biography written by his daughter.

in the 1840s even some of the more remote parts of Ireland had regular coaching services, such as those which ran from Tralee and Killarney to Cork.

The most famous name from this coaching era is that of Charles Bianconi, an emigrant from Italy who settled in County Tipperary. He began as an itinerant print seller, but moved on to start his first coach service, between Clonmel and Cahir, in 1815. By 1840 his coaches served most of Munster, Connaught and Leinster, offering fares of as little one and a half pence per mile, and running at speeds on good roads of up to 8mph. By the mid-1840s, Bianconi had one hundred cars covering around 3,500 miles a day.

As well as its roads, by 1830 Ireland had a network of some 600 miles of canals and navigable rivers. The most notable were the Grand and Royal Canals, which linked Dublin to the Shannon. There was a long branch off the Grand Canal to Athy, where it met the Barrow Navigation, part canal and

Old meets new in West Dublin – the Red Line of the LUAS tram system crosses the Ann Devlin Bridge over the Royal Canal near Suir Road station (irishwaterwayshistory.com).

part river navigation, linking Dublin to Waterford. In Ulster the Lagan Navigation ran from Belfast to Lough Neagh, and the ill-fated and unsuccessful Ulster Canal joined Lough Neagh to Lough Erne. Finished in 1841 at a cost of £231,000, the locks on the Ulster Canal were three feet narrower than those of the canals linked to it. Within a few decades of its opening it was virtually redundant, seen off by Ulster's railways. Also in Ulster, the Newry Canal had opened as long ago as 1742, built to bring coal from the pits in east Tyrone around Coalisland to

The daily Bianconi goods wagon setting out from Hearn's Hotel in Clonmel; a four-horse Bianconi fast carriage (opposite).

Irish roadmenders, 1820s, by an unknown artist.

the coast at Newry for onward transit to warm the hearths in the growing city of Dublin.

As early as the 1820s it was clear that indigenous Irish industries were struggling in competition with the most powerful industrial force on the planet, which lay just across the Irish Sea. When the Act of Union abolishing the Irish parliament was passed in 1800, in effect a free trade area was created between the two countries. The parliament at Westminster allowed some exceptions to this in the form of protective duties on leather, glass, furniture, woollen and cotton goods, but other industries left exposed to market forces, such as the making of silk, quickly perished.

A Bianconi day car (above).

Two Bianconi four-horse standard carriages (opposite).

William Huskisson, later to become the world's first celebrity rail accident victim when he was killed on the opening day of the Liverpool and Manchester Railway in September 1830, together with other advocates of free trade, abolished these protective tariffs in 1824, leaving Irish industries extremely vulnerable. As the railway network spread into almost every part of the country later in the century, rather than being a force for economic regeneration, paradoxically it often made it easier for the mass-produced products of British factories to compete with locally-made goods. With the exception of north-east Ulster, Ireland was more dependent on subsistence agriculture at the end of the nineteenth century than it was at the beginning. As an example of this process, in 1815, in Bandon in County Cork, there were 2,000 weavers at work on their looms. By 1840 they numbered just 150.

Ireland on the eve of the railway age had a very good network of roads and canals. There were a number of cities and large towns, and some signs of British-style industrial development in Ulster. There was an adequate banking and exchange system, and in the wake of Catholic Emancipation in 1829 a considerable measure of political stability. The population was large and growing, but there was no inevitability about what was to happen in the 1840s. All in all, the Ireland of the 1830s seemed an excellent place to promote the railway, the new wonder of the industrial age.

Chapter 2

THE DAWN OF THE RAILWAY AGE

1834–1850

Ireland's first railway, the Dublin and Kingstown, was promoted by a group of wealthy and influential Dublin businessmen and bankers – serious, hard-headed, visionary and powerful men. A leading figure was the banker James Pim, who became the treasurer of the company in May 1832 and gave it effective leadership for many years. On his death in 1856, a eulogy written by the directors of the D&K stated that his exertions on behalf of the company had been of national benefit in that he drew public notice to the advantages of railway communication and encouraged many people in Ireland to promote railways.

The eminent Irish engineer Charles Blacker Vignoles was appointed to carry the scheme through, and a loan of £75,000 was secured from the Board of Public Works. The capital of the company was set at £150,000, and the contract to build the line, which was just over five miles in length, was given to a man who was to become a major figure in the construction of the Irish railway network, William Dargan. Built to a gauge of 4ft 8½in, this line, the first public railway in Ireland, opened on 17 December 1834.

Dublin and Kingstown Railway, pavilions at Lord Cloncurry's Demesne of Maratimo near Blackrock, an 1840 engraving by Andrew Nicholl (National Library of Ireland).

This modest beginning to the railway age in Ireland should be seen in context. In 1835, only 330 miles of railway were in operation across the Irish Sea. Ireland now had its foot on the ladder. We should look back respectfully on the far-sightedness of these early railway promoters. Railways were still at a very early stage in their development, and much of the technology they used was virtually untested. Building a railway anywhere in the early 1830s, let alone in Ireland, was a risky and expensive venture. Many influential people were still unconvinced by this radical new technology. Though the wind was beginning to turn and favour the spread of railways, there were still many pitfalls along the road for those involved in the first railway schemes.

The mid-1830s saw the first of two intense bouts of speculation in railway stocks which have become known to history as 'the railway manias'. The success of the world's first railway linking two major cities, the Liverpool and Manchester, which opened in 1830, showed that a railway on a large scale was both viable and profitable. Political stability in the wake of the great Reform Act of 1832 and improving economic conditions encouraged the promotion of a large number of railway schemes throughout Britain.

Ireland followed the trend, with hundreds of miles of railway being promoted. A number of these were hugely overambitious or improbably expensive. One such scheme was put forward by the Grand Atlantic Railroad Company, which intended to raise £2.4 million to build a railway from Dublin to the west of Ireland serving Galway, Sligo and Castlebar. Another was the plan for a railway from Dublin to Valentia in County Kerry, where a new port would be built to serve transatlantic shipping. Passengers and mail could then travel by rail across Ireland, and reach Britain and the rest of Europe more quickly than if they concluded their journey by sea. This idea of a great railway-served port in the west was an Irish vision of an El Dorado which kept popping up throughout the nineteenth century.

Some of the key components in what would become, in time, a truly national network were first promoted at this time. The Great Leinster and Munster Railway Company was formed to obtain an Act to build a line between Dublin and Cork. A line from Dublin to Drogheda was first proposed in a pamphlet published in April 1835 by Thomas Brodigan, a landowner who lived near Drogheda. In November of that year, the Belfast newspaper, the *Northern Whig*, announced the formation of a company prophetically called the Grand Northern Irish Railway, whose aim was the building of a railway from Belfast to Armagh and then extending the line further to the west.

As well as the not unreasonable desire to make money, many of the promoters of these early schemes were motivated by the idea that railways represented

LOCOMOTIVE ENGINE—DUBLIN AND KINSTOWN RAILWAY

Hibernia, one of the first steam locomotives to run in Ireland, was supplied for the opening of the Dublin and Kingstown Railway in 1834.

progress, the spirit of the age. As early as the mid-1830s this new mode of transportation was being seen as the mark of true civilisation; not having a network of railways in Ireland would mark the country as a backwater lagging behind the rest of the nation. This was often expressed in florid and even bombastic language. The *Northern Whig*, at times behaving almost as the house magazine of the Ulster Railway Company, in 1835 described its embryonic scheme as 'one of those great movements to which we have longingly looked forward, when the province of Ulster, then the whole of Ireland, shaking free of her inglorious thralldom, would spring up into fresh and healthy vigour, and secure for her children the just character of a wise, a rich, enterprising and happy people.'

Despite the many companies promoted in the mid-1830s and the great hopes invested in them, the only railway schemes launched in that first Irish

The Dublin and Drogheda Railway at Baldoyle Bridge, an 1846 engraving.

railway mania that actually went on to build their lines were the Dublin and Drogheda Railway and the Ulster Railway. These two companies were to operate the northern and southern extremities of what later became the main line between Dublin and Belfast.

Railway promotion was inextricably linked to the overall state of the national economy. Good economic conditions had sparked the mania in the first place, and it took little more than a bad harvest in 1836 to deflate it again. As the economic cycle turned, confidence began to ebb away. There was a financial crisis and a slowdown in trade and commerce. Failure of the Agricultural and Commercial Bank severely hit investor confidence, and many of the railway schemes which had been filling the papers with their advertisements and prospectuses

were quietly dropped. On 1 August the Marquis of Lansdowne announced in the House of Lords that a commission was to be established 'to appoint proper persons to inquire and report upon the most advantageous lines of railway in Ireland.'

The immediate effect of the appointment of the Commissioners on a General System of Railways for Ireland was to create even further uncertainty in an already jittery market. The commission was given the task of planning a system of railways for the whole of Ireland, and railway promoters and speculators were immediately concerned that their particular schemes might not have a role in any government-planned and possibly officially-sponsored national network.

The appointment of the Commissioners was radical for the time. In an age of *laissez faire* and largely unregulated capitalism, the government appeared to be proposing to plan a national network for Ireland.

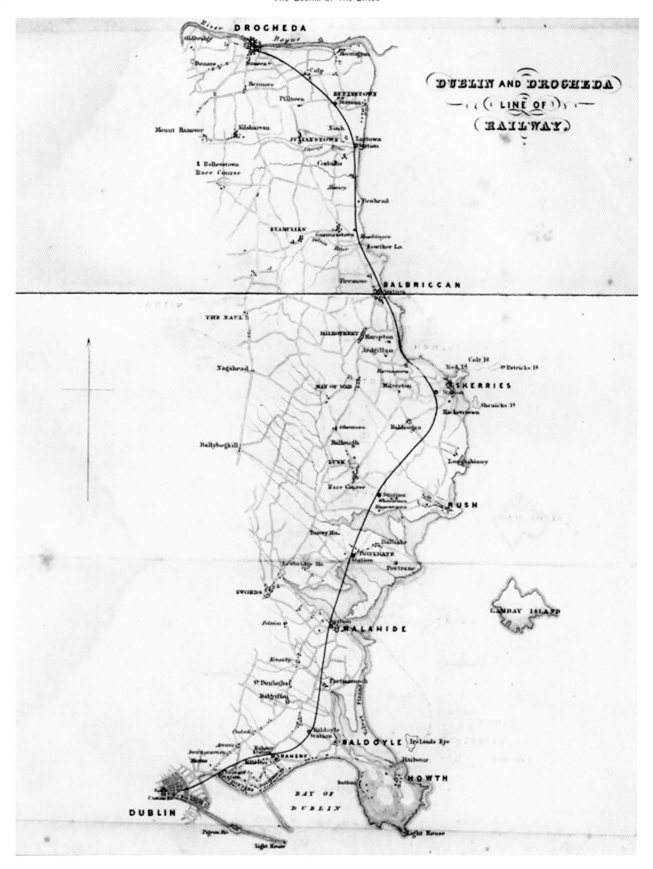

The Dublin and Drogheda Railway: the terminus at Drogheda (above) in an 1846 engraving, and the map of the route (opposite).

Yet even the most doctrinaire non-interventionists realised that the new railways had to be controlled and regulated in some way. The chaos in the south of England caused by the use of different gauges was becoming ever more apparent, especially where Brunel's Great Western Railway with its 7ft gauge made a junction with other lines built to standard or 4ft 8½in gauge. The government hoped that Ireland would be spared these problems, for as well as drawing up a plan for a national network the Irish Railway Commissioners were also asked to recommend the standard gauge to be used in Ireland.

In terms of its contribution to the development of railways in Ireland, the Commission was a failure, but its report and atlas are a fabulous resource for the historian. The Commissioners conducted a detailed economic and social survey of the country, a window on an Ireland that was soon to disappear under the ravages of the Great Famine and the depopulation which followed. When it was published in 1838 the final report of the Irish Railway Commissioners provided a detailed economic survey of the condition of Ireland at that time, even down to an analysis of the traffic flows on existing roads and canals. Though the report was generally pessimistic about the potential prosperity of railways in Ireland, it did recommend the construction of two trunk routes from Dublin, one heading north-west and the other south-west, together with branches off these main lines. It also proposed a cross-country line from Limerick to Waterford. There was no recommendation for a line from Dublin to the west coast, the Commissioners believing that the existing Royal and Grand Canals were adequate for the available traffic.

Lisburn station in about 1905, a colour postcard.

It had been hoped that the network suggested by the Commissioners would be supported by government money. Their conclusion, that railways in Ireland could not be funded by conventional methods, led to them seeing Irish railways as public works backed by state funding rather than commercial enterprises. In reality there was never any chance that the government would provide money to back the Commissioners' plans, so a great opportunity to create a properly-planned national system of railways for Ireland was lost before it had even begun to be built. The Commissioners' pessimistic view of the difficulties of financing railway building in Ireland was proven to be correct all too often in the decades that followed. The only part of the Commissioners' report that was acted upon was its recommendation as to the gauge which should be used in Ireland – 6ft 2in. In the event, only the Ulster Railway adopted this gauge, a decision which, as we will see, was to cause major problems in the next decade.

The only railway which actually opened for business in the 1830s, on 12 August 1839, was the first short section of the Ulster Railway from Belfast to Lisburn. Such was the novelty of the affair that around 3,000 passengers were carried on the first day and many more were turned away. Proceedings were slightly marred by the derailment of one of the engines at the Belfast terminus.

An improvement in economic conditions in the mid-1840s led to a second bout of railway mania, and this time it delivered the spine of the national network in Ireland. As an indication of just how much activity was going on at this time, in 1846 alone seventy-eight Irish railway bills were presented to parliament. Some of these were highly speculative and very costly, such as the Kilrush, Dublin and Belfast Junction Railway, which hoped to raise £1.5 million to link the small port of Kilrush on the Shannon Estuary in County Clare with the country's two largest cities.

Only four decades separate *Hibernia* (page 30) and this locomotive, GNR 0–4–2 No. 106 *Tornado*, originally built for the Ulster Railway in the early 1870s. The two images show how rapidly the steam locomotive developed in such a short space of time.

The 1840s saw the opening of much of what was to become the line linking Ireland's two largest cities, Dublin and Belfast. The Ulster Railway had extended its line to Portadown by 1842, though its intention had always been to head westwards to Armagh and beyond rather than south towards Dublin. The Dublin and Drogheda opened what would eventually be the southern part of the Dublin–Belfast main line in 1844. A new company, the Dublin and Belfast Junction Railway, formed to fill the 55-mile gap between Drogheda and Portadown, obtained its Act in 1845.

The core of Ulster's railway network was also started in the 1840s. The UR completed the line set out in its original 1835 prospectus when its trains began to run to Armagh on 1 March 1848. Back in 1836, in the frenzy of schemes being promoted at the time, a prospectus had been published for the Londonderry and Enniskillen Railway. This line was to link the towns in its title, via Strabane and Omagh. The route was surveyed in 1837 by George Stephenson, but with the worsening economic conditions of the late 1830s the scheme was not pursued. It was revived in 1845, and the first section from Derry to Strabane opened in April 1847.

On the east coast, two companies were promoted to provide lines which would branch off the D&BJR route – the Dundalk and Enniskillen and the Newry and Enniskillen. The first section of the D&E, from a station at Barrack Street in Dundalk to Castleblayney, opened on the same day as D&BJ services to Dundalk began – 15 February 1849. The location of the D&E's station, to the east of the main line, meant that its trains had to cross the Dublin line on the level. The painfully slow expansion of both the D&E and L&E to an eventual junction at Enniskillen belongs to the next chapter, and while they did both eventually achieve their original objectives, the same could not be said

Brunel in Ireland

Perhaps the best known engineer of the Victorian era was Isambard Kingdom Brunel. Although small in stature, in every other way he was larger than life. His achievements are the stuff of drama and legend: from the largest ships of his era to the Great Western Railway built to his own unique 7ft gauge which first linked London and Bristol, then crossed the Severn to enter south Wales. It was the affairs of the South Wales Railway which brought him to Ireland. This line was a satellite of the GWR and, like many of the great Victorian railways which served the west coast of Britain, it had its eye on the potentially lucrative traffic on the Irish Sea. In the 1840s the SWR planned an ambitious scheme to extend the 7ft gauge beyond Swansea to a new port in west Wales at Fishguard. From here, steamers would take passengers and goods across to Ireland to another new port which was to be constructed south of Wexford on the shores of Greenore Bay. Much later this would become known as Rosslare. A railway was planned to connect this port to Dublin, running up the east coast through Wexford and reaching the Irish capital over the existing tracks of the Dublin and Kingstown line. A new company backed by the GWR was formed. This had the cumbersome name of the Waterford, Wexford, Wicklow and Dublin Railway, and obtained its Act of Parliament in July 1846.

It was in the planning of this railway that Brunel made his mark on Ireland. There were two possible routes south from Bray. The most obvious was inland following the same course as the main road from Dublin to Wexford takes to this day. Perhaps this was too conventional

Isambard Kingdom Brunel by the launching chains of the *Great Eastern*, the famous photograph taken in 1857 by Robert Howlett.

for Brunel, who saw that a more direct route was one that followed the coast, even if this meant that his railway had to be taken through or round Bray Head. He surveyed the route and construction began in August 1848, though the line through to Wicklow was not completed until 1855. To this day the run from Bray to Greystones is one of the most spectacular railway journeys in Ireland. Brunel's original alignment

A contemporary engraving of the Ram's Scalp Bridge accident, August 1867.

took the line through several tunnels and across inlets of the sea on the great engineer's flimsy looking but sturdy trademark wooden viaducts. However, the price which those who inherited the route had to pay, from the 1850s through to today, was constant vigilance as the alignment was lashed by storms and rock falls.

It was the scene of several accidents, the most serious of which occurred on 9 August 1867 when a derailment as it crossed the Ram's Scalp Bridge led to the engine and all but the last carriage of a train from Enniscorthy plunging about thirty feet down the ravine, killing two passengers and injuring twenty-three others.

Subsequent generations of railway engineers have gradually edged the line away from the sea and observant travellers today will see traces of Brunel's original formation which have been abandoned, including the abutments where his viaducts once carried the line over the water.

Even when it reached the relative sanctuary of Greystones, the line south, though level, was so close to the coast it was often subject to inundations and washouts caused by the sea. I am sure that many of those tasked with the maintenance of the line over the past 160 years have often wished that it had been laid out by an engineer who was less of a visionary than Brunel and that it had taken the more practical inland route to link Dublin with Wicklow, Wexford and Rosslare.

The Atmospheric Railway

For a brief time in the 1840s, the short stretch of railway, less than two miles long, between Kingstown and Dalkey was seen to be at the cutting edge of railway science, offering, as it appeared to do, an alternative to the steam locomotive. There are few reminders of this audacious experiment left today, but there is a lane in Dalkey called Atmospheric Road, which gives a clue as to what the directors of the D&K were doing over 160 years ago.

We all know from the rudiments of science we have retained from our schooldays that nature abhors a vacuum. It was suggested as early as the seventeenth century that if a vacuum could be created and then broken, the inrush of air could propel a vehicle. The original concept seems to have envisaged some sort of vehicle in a large tube from which the air would be sucked, but this was later refined by a British inventor called Samuel Clegg to a railway carriage with a piston which was inserted into a large pipe between the rails. The pipe was sealed with a leather flap which closed behind the passage of the train, so maintaining the vacuum in the pipe, which was created by pumping stations built at intervals alongside the track.

Clegg's invention was taken up by a firm of London engineers, the Samuda Brothers, and a demonstration line was built in London in 1840. The system was called the atmospheric railway, and among the visitors who came to see it at

work was James Pim and some of his fellow directors of the D&K. They had been thinking of extending their line to Dalkey along the route of the tramway which had been built to bring stone down to Kingstown to build the harbour. They bravely, or insanely, decided to apply the atmospheric system to the Dalkey extension. The extension was separate from the original D&K, so through running from Dublin to Dalkey was not possible.

The 15-inch diameter cast iron pipe, in which the vacuum was created, lay between the rails. The leather seal on the top of the pipe, which was critical to the success of the whole operation, was held in place by iron plates rivetted to the pipe and lubricated with tallow to keep it supple. If

Arriving at Kingstown on the Atmospheric Railway, *The Illustrated London News*, 6 January 1844.

the seal was not immediately restored following the passage of a train, air would be admitted to the pipe and, in extreme cases, the system would not work. If it leaked, the steam engines at the pumping station, which extracted the air from the pipe and were located near the Dalkey terminus, had to work harder, burning more coal in the process. The line was uphill nearly all the way from Kingstown to Dalkey, so atmospheric traction was only required in that direction; the trains free-wheeled back to Kingstown.

The line opened in March 1844, with trains running every half hour. Clegg and his backers took no royalties on their patents. The Dalkey line was to be a practical application of their system used to demonstrate and ultimately sell the atmospheric railway principle to other interested parties. Many eminent visitors came to see it, including Isambard Kingdom Brunel, who was so taken with it that he later applied the system to the South Devon Railway on which he was the engineer. Undoubtedly, the atmospheric system could cope with stiffer gradients than the steam locomotives of the 1840s, so to this day the legacy of Brunel's flirtation with the atmospheric railway is a line with steep inclines, not much of a problem for today's diesels, but a nightmare for operators throughout the age of steam.

The practical difficulties of maintaining the vacuum in the pipe were beyond the technology and materials of the time. The Dalkey line lasted as an atmospheric railway until April 1854 when it was closed to be rebuilt as a conventional railway when the line was extended to Bray and beyond by the Dublin and Wicklow company. The system was used for longer by the D&K than in Devon and on the London and Croydon Railway, the other applications in Britain. However, in the end, this proved to be a blind alley in terms of the development of railways and left the steam locomotive unchallenged as the main motive power for the world's railways until it was displaced by diesel and electric traction in the second half of the last century.

Atmospheric Road, Dalkey, a tangible reminder in the twenty-first century of the radical railway experiment conducted here in the 1840s.

An Ulster Railway excursion to Belfast on 16 September 1852, painted by an unknown artist, probably at the UR's Great Victoria Street terminus.

for the third line started on the east coast at this time, the Newry and Enniskillen.

Two Newry-based railways were promoted in the mid-1840s. One of these, the Newry, Warrenpoint and Rostrevor, was a short local line authorised in 1846, which opened in 1849 between Newry and Warrenpoint – it never reached Rostrevor. The other company, the N&E, had a more chequered history. Authorised by an Act of Parliament in July 1845, the company planned a line over seventy miles long to reach Enniskillen via Armagh and Clones. Parliament insisted that the section from Enniskillen to Clones should be built first, in collaboration with the D&E. Construction began in 1846 on a short line less than four miles in length, from Newry to a junction of the D&BJ at Goraghwood. While the speed of construction on some Irish lines at this time is mentioned elsewhere, incredibly this short stretch of track did not open until March 1854.

Further north, two other significant schemes were being promoted. The Belfast and County Down Railway was incorporated by an Act in January 1846 to build a main line from Belfast to Downpatrick, with a branch to Holywood on the shores of Belfast Lough.

Kilcummer Viaduct on the GS&WR Fermoy Branch which opened in 1860, painted by Robert Stopford in 1862.

The Holywood line opened in August 1848 with the first section of the B&CDR main line, as far as Comber, following in May 1850. The first parts of what was to become an extensive system of lines serving much of the counties of Antrim and Londonderry were built by the Belfast & Ballymena Railway Company. This was another scheme which had first been proposed in the 1830s and was revived during the following decade. Authorised in 1845, by 1848 lines had been opened from its station at York Road in Belfast to serve Carrickfergus, Ballymena and Randalstown.

By far the most significant company to be promoted in the early 1840s was the Great Southern and Western Railway, which was formed to build a great trunk line to the south and west to link Dublin, Limerick and Cork. The company needed to raise capital of £1,300,000, but its shares were quickly taken up. The GS&WR's Act was passed by parliament in 1844, and with considerable ceremony the first sod was cut by the Duke of Leinster, at Adamstown near Lucan in January 1845. The first part of the GS&WR to open was a branch to Carlow, which diverged from the main line at Cherryville Junction near Kildare. Services began on the fifty-five-mile-long line to Carlow in August 1846, though a shortage of rolling stock meant that, at first, only two trains ran daily. Meanwhile, work progressed on the main line, with trains serving Maryborough (Portlaoise) from June 1847 and Ballybrophy in September of that year. The £600,000 contract for the final section of the line, the seventy-eight miles from Thurles to Cork, was given to William Dargan, who had already built sections of the GS&WR line closer to Dublin.

Trains began to run as far as Thurles in March 1848. Limerick Junction was reached in July 1848 and Mallow, 144 miles from Dublin, in March 1849. GS&WR trains finally served the temporary station at Blackpool, on the outskirts of Cork, from 29 October 1849. This remained the terminus until 1855, when work was completed on the 1,335-yard-long tunnel which brought the line into the city at Penrose Quay. The line from Dublin to that temporary Cork terminus was just over 160 miles long. At that time it was the longest line in the British Isles – it had been built in its entirety in under five years by a workforce that had no experience of railway construction, against the background of the social and economic catastrophe which was the Great Famine. The company had some government assistance in the form of a loan of half a million pounds, but it had also had to deal with the effects of the terrible results of hunger, disease and social breakdown. In the circumstances the construction of such a long railway in such a short time was an astonishing achievement.

The surge of railway promotion in the 1840s saw other lines come out of lengthy hibernation. The Waterford and Limerick Railway was authorised in July 1845, a revival of the first Irish railway to obtain an Act of Parliament in 1826. A provisional committee was formed in Waterford in 1844 with Charles Vignoles as engineer. To build the line, via Carrick-on-Suir, Clonmel and Tipperary, capital of £750,000 had to be raised. The W&L was to cross the GS&WR near

Tipperary at that famous location known ever since as Limerick Junction. It actually got there ahead of the GS&WR, with goods and passenger services running between Limerick and Tipperary in April and May 1848, respectively. Thereafter progress was slow, the line to Waterford not being completed until 1854.

The Irish Railway Commissioners had taken the view that a railway from Dublin to the west of Ireland would not be viable, and while the initial plans of the GS&WR included a line to Galway this was not pursued. This change of plans led to the resignation of several members of the provisional committee, led by John Ennis, who set up a scheme of their own to build a line to the west under the title of the Midland Great Western Railway. The MGWR Act of July 1845 authorised the company to raise £1 million to build a line from Dublin to Mullingar and Longford. In a moment of inspiration, the company bought the Royal Canal and built its railway alongside it.

The Lord Lieutenant turned the first sod on 12 January 1846 at the site of the company's Dublin terminus at the Broadstone in Phibsboro. As with the GS&WR line, construction proceeded with remarkable speed. The engineer, George Willoughby Hemans, reported to the board in September 1846 that fifteen miles of track had already been laid and ballasted.

Chapter 3

CONSOLIDATION AND EXPANSION

1850–1880

The years between 1850 and 1880 saw a rapid expansion of Ireland's railway network. By the end of this period the railway had reached into most parts of the country, promoted and financed largely in the established manner. If all went to plan a company was floated, an act of parliament was obtained, and the finance was then raised. A recurring theme throughout this period, especially in relation to the smaller companies and those operating in the more remote parts of the country, was the difficulty they had in raising enough capital to complete their lines through the sale of shares. Though the government, through the agency of the Public Works Loan Commissioners, provided some help in the form of loans to railway companies, these carried interest charges and had to be repaid.

The three companies whose lines would serve most of the province of Ulster were all running train services by the end of the 1840s. The tracks of the Belfast and Ballymena Railway, which had been incorporated in 1845, had reached Carrickfergus, Ballymena and Randalstown by 1848. The Randalstown line was extended to Cookstown in County Tyrone in 1856. In the north-west, another line incorporated in

1845, the Londonderry and Coleraine, was making much slower progress. Construction did not begin until the 1850s. It reached Limavady in 1852 and was completed from what became Limavady Junction to Coleraine in 1853. To bridge the gap between Coleraine and Ballymena, a company was floated in 1853 with one of the longest names in Irish railway history – the Ballymena, Ballymoney, Coleraine and Portrush Junction Railway. Construction of its thirty-four-mile line between Ballymena and Portrush was accomplished quickly, and it opened in December 1855. At Coleraine the respective stations of the L&C and the BBC&P were on opposite sides of the River Bann, and through running was not possible until the river was bridged in 1860. Another impediment to trains running from Belfast to Londonderry was that they had to reverse at Greenisland, on the line to Carrickfergus, before heading north. This was because the locomotives of this early period were unable to cope with the severe gradients a more direct route would have entailed, and this remained the case until the 1930s when a direct line was eventually built.

In 1860 the B&B changed its name to the Belfast and Northern Counties Railway, and started a bold plan of consolidation and expansion. The following year the B&NCR acquired the BBC&PJ and leased the

Dundalk, Newry and Greenore 0–6–0ST No. 4 *Newry* at Carlingford, *c.*1878, a painting by Norman Whitla.

REPORT OF THE DIRECTORS

TO

THE SHAREHOLDERS

OF THE

BELFAST AND BALLYMENA RAILWAY COMPANY,

AT THE

FOURTEENTH HALF-YEARLY GENERAL MEETING, 29TH MAY, 1852.

YOUR Directors present to the Proprietors a Statement of the Half-Year's Traffic.

The Receipts from 12,998 First Class Passengers,			£1,603 15 10
" " 42,746 Second Class do.,			3,455 16 10
" " 122,568 Third Class do.,			3,374 18 1
178,312			£8,434 10 9
For Parcels,	£332 11 8		
" Horses,	27 3 6		
" Carriages,	17 7 4		
" Dogs,	12 15 9		
			389 18 3
			£8,824 9 0
Cartage,	229 0 10		
" Rents,	23 12 6		
" Transfer Fees,	10 2 6		
			262 15 10
Goods,			6,157 9 1
Mails,			496 10 9
			£15,741 4 8

IN reviewing the Traffic of the Half-year, and contrasting it with the previous corresponding Half-year, we find a decrease of 2,549 First-Class Passengers, but an increase in the receipts from this Class of £51 5s 10d, thereby shewing that the Passengers have travelled a greater distance, although fewer in number, inasmuch as there has been no alteration in the fares; and, in the Second Class, a decrease of 12,801 Passengers, with only a falling off in the receipts of £147 3s 1d. In the Third Class, an increase of 25,942 Passengers, and in amount £507 11s 1d.

L&C, taking it over ten years later in 1871. In May 1860 parliament authorised the Carrickfergus and Larne Railway to build a fourteen-mile line from Carrick to Larne Harbour. This was nominally a separate company, but the line was worked by the B&NCR from its opening in 1862, which was also the year in which steamer services began to run between Larne and Stranraer in Scotland. The final addition to the B&NCR system in this period was also built by an independent company, the Derry Central Railway. This line diverged from the B&NCR Cookstown branch at Magherafelt, and ran for twenty-nine miles through a largely rural district with no major towns, roughly parallel to, but to the west of, the River Bann, to meet the B&NCR main line at Macfin Junction, three miles from Coleraine.

The first page of the 1852 *Directors' Report* of the Belfast and Ballymena Railway Company (Ian Dinmore collection).

The Derry Central opened throughout in February 1880 and was worked from the outset by the B&NCR, who acquired the company in 1895.

The first part of the compact system which was to serve County Down opened in August 1848. This was a line from Belfast to Holywood operated by the Belfast and County Down Railway, authorised by an act passed in January 1846. The B&CDR's main line branched off the Holywood line just outside its Belfast terminus, and was opened as far as Comber in May 1850. Though a branch from Comber to Newtownards was opened in 1850, the main line was not extended to Downpatrick until 1859. A short branch of three and a half miles served Ballynahinch from 1858.

The prospect of substantial cross-channel traffic between Donaghadee and Portpatrick in Galloway encouraged the company to extend its Newtownards branch to Donaghadee in 1861, but in the event steamers only ran from Portpatrick to Donaghadee for two years before they transferred to Stranraer and Larne. By this time the B&CDR was close to bankruptcy and needed a government loan of £160,000 to keep it afloat. With its flawed focus on the potential honeypot of traffic through Donaghadee, a much more obvious extension, extending the Holywood line to the growing town of Bangor, was overlooked. In 1860 a separate company, the Belfast, Holywood and Bangor Railway, built this line, which opened in 1865. It eventually came into the B&CDR fold, and today is the only part of the system which is still open. The B&CDR finally completed its main line to the seaside resort of Newcastle in 1869.

For nearly three quarters of a century the railway system in the rest of Ulster was dominated by the Great Northern Railway, established in 1876, though much water had flowed down the Lagan, Foyle and Boyne before the GNR came on the scene. The first major piece in an often complicated jigsaw was the completion of the line between Dublin and Belfast. To achieve this, two of the iconic set pieces of the Irish railway network had to be completed by the D&BJR: the majestic eighteen-arch Craigmore Viaduct near Newry, the highest on the Irish railway network, and the viaduct spanning the River Boyne at Drogheda. In addition, trains in both directions had to face a stiff climb to a summit at milepost 65½ near Newry, so this was not an easy line to build or operate.

The first section, from a temporary terminus at Newfoundwell just north of Drogheda to Dundalk,

The majestic arches of the Craigmore Viaduct against a threatening sky (D. Mull).

The Disaster at Straffan

Today, travelling by train is one of the safest forms of transport there is, but this is largely because of lessons learned, often the hard way, over the last two centuries. Though the safety record of Irish railways compares well with other countries in western Europe, accidents did happen, and in the course of this book we will look at four of the most significant of these accidents. The first casts light on the hazardous way that railways were run in their early years.

As railways began to spread rapidly across Britain and Ireland in the 1840s, there were no precedents to follow as to how they should be managed and operated. In an age when the dominant political ethos was *laissez-faire*, there was little direction or regulation; railway companies had to work systems out for themselves as they went along. Though slow in comparison with today's trains, the early railways still ran at speeds much greater than had ever been possible before. Mechanical failures such as broken axles and boiler explosions were not uncommon. There were also many injuries and numerous fatalities among railway workers as, often unaware of the dangers their work presented, they were run down by speeding trains or crushed between vehicles. The relatively slow speeds of the early locomotives disguised the perils inherent in early operating practices, and a serious accident was bound to happen sooner or later. The events which unfolded at Straffan on the GS&WR on the evening of 5 October 1853 caused the greatest number of fatalities in an Irish railway accident up to that time.

As the light faded that autumn evening, fog shrouded this part of Kildare. A passenger train

which had left Cork at midday had just passed through Straffan station when a piston rod broke, damaging one of the locomotive's cylinders. The train came to a halt 974 yards from the station on the Dublin side. There were forty-five passengers in the train's five carriages.

Breakdowns of this kind were not uncommon, and the train and its passengers were in no immediate danger. Rudimentary measures were made to protect the train. The guard sent a GS&WR pay clerk who was travelling on the train back with a red flag, and he stuck the flag into the ground 300 yards from the rear of the train before returning. There was no tail lamp on the train, and the guard made no attempt to protect it with detonators or fog signals, which would have exploded under the wheels of an approaching train, thus warning the driver of an obstruction ahead.

The failed passenger train had been stationary for some twenty minutes when it was struck in the rear by a goods train travelling at an estimated 30mph. As a result of the violent collision, eighteen people lost their lives.

At the coroner's inquest, blame for the crash was placed on the driver and fireman of the goods train, but in their annual return of accidents the Board of Trade put a different complexion on the matter, reporting that, 'a want of break (sic) power, an inadequate supply of signals, inefficient regulations, and a defective system for securing a proper interval between trains, were combined with negligence in the inferior servants, to produce the accident.'

The inspecting officer's report casts a fascinating light on some of the operating practices of the time. He noted that the guard had only one small red hand lamp to protect the stranded passenger train, although there should have been three red lights to show at its rear at night. The appropriate lights were not aboard the train at the time of the accident; they should have been sent down from Dublin to be put on the train at Kildare, but the stationmaster at Kildare had failed to do this and the guard had not noticed their absence. There were, however, two powerful red lights burning on the front of the failed engine. If these been brought to the rear of the train the driver of the approaching goods vehicle, which the train staff knew was coming, would have seen them and might have stopped in time.

A further problem was that the buffers on the goods engine were at a different height to those on the passenger carriages. This meant that, on collision, the buffers on the two vehicles did not absorb any of the impact of the engine and its 177-ton goods train. The engine of the goods train ploughed into the rear passenger carriage unchecked, completely demolishing it. The inspecting officer also found that instructions issued by the company to its staff were ambiguous and misleading, and that there was insufficient braking power on the goods train to stop it quickly in an emergency.

A key element of railway practice at this time – and for many years afterwards – was the time interval system. A train was allowed to follow the previous working train after the passage of what was deemed to be sufficient time for the first train to be well out of its way. A slow goods train might follow a faster passenger train after, say, ten minutes had elapsed, while a fast train would not be allowed to follow a slow goods train until perhaps twenty minutes had passed. This was fine as long as the train in front did not break down, as happened at Straffan, but it was a potentially dangerous way to run a railway. Over the next thirty-six years the railway inspectors of the Board of Trade pointed this out many times in the course of their investigations into accidents. They also constantly recommended improved braking systems for trains. On both counts they were largely ignored by the railway companies and the legislators. This changed suddenly and dramatically in 1889, when another and much more serious accident forced drastic changes.

opened in February 1849, and was extended to a remote temporary station at Wellington Inn, just north of the present-day border, in July 1850. With the completion of Craigmore Viaduct in 1852, trains from Newfoundwell could run through to Portadown and on to Belfast over the tracks of the UR.

Through running between Belfast and Dublin was impossible until the Boyne Viaduct at Drogheda was completed. A temporary timber viaduct was replaced by an iron lattice work structure which opened in April 1855. The viaduct led to a row between Sir John Macneill and his former pupil, James Barton, the first engineering graduate from Trinity College, who had worked for Macneill. Barton had the temerity to claim that it was he and not Macneill who had designed the viaduct, though Macneill claimed much of the credit.

In 1853 a branch to Navan, originally promoted by the D&BJR but now in the hands of the D&D, was extended to Kells, twenty-six miles from Drogheda. This line was extended a further thirteen miles to reach Oldcastle in 1863.

In 1849 another future component of the GNR, the first section of the Dundalk and Enniskillen Railway, opened from Dundalk as far as Castleblayney. Thereafter progress was slow, and several return visits to parliament were required to renew lapsed powers before Ballybay was reached in 1854, Newbliss in 1855, Clones in 1858, and finally Enniskillen in 1859. A short eight-mile branch from Shantonagh Junction

The Boyne Viaduct at Drogheda on a summer's day in 2006 (Wikimedia Commons).

to Cootehill opened in 1860, but the D&E's finances did not permit its intended extension to Cavan.

At Enniskillen the D&E made a junction with the Londonderry and Enniskillen, which had reached the Fermanagh town in 1854. Like so many Irish companies, the L&E struggled to raise the capital to build its line, taking seven years to construct sixty miles of track. The L&E's pecuniary embarrassment was indirectly responsible for one of the great oddities of the Irish railway network. When the line reached the small County Tyrone village of Fintona in 1853, construction stopped for about a year whilst the company scraped up funds to continue towards Enniskillen.

The Fintona horse tram during its last days of operation in 1957 (RMWeb).

When work resumed the following year, it was decided to carry on towards Enniskillen from a point about a mile from the village, leaving Fintona at the end of a very short branch. To work the line from Fintona Junction to Fintona economically, the company was permitted to use horse traction; from then until the closure of the line in 1957 the branch was the preserve of the Fintona horse tram. The tram's motive power was a series of geldings, all of which were called Dick. The tram survives, and can be seen at the Ulster Folk and Transport Museum at Cultra.

The L&E had just two branch lines. The Finn Valley Railway from Strabane to Stranorlar opened in 1863 as a broad gauge line, but was converted to 3ft gauge in 1894. The other was a thirty-five-mile line from Bundoran Junction, eight miles north of Enniskillen, to Bundoran on the Atlantic coast at the southern tip of County Donegal. This was built by an independent company, the Enniskillen, Bundoran and Sligo. Its name reflected the intention to extend the railway the twenty or so miles to Sligo, but the extension, authorised in 1862, was never built. Had it been completed there would have been a railway down the whole west coast of Ireland from Derry to Limerick, and given the money spent building speculative projects elsewhere in the country it is a great shame this link was never built.

One line in this part of the world which never became part of the GNR was the Sligo, Leitrim and Northern Counties Railway, linking Enniskillen and Sligo via Manorhamilton. The SL&NCR, authorised

RAILWAY STATION, CLONES. *No 220*

Clones station in a postcard of around 1910.

in 1875 with a share capital of £200,000 and additional powers to borrow up to £100,000, reached Sligo at its western end through running powers over five miles of the MGWR from its junction with the SL&NCR at Carrignagat. The line from Enniskillen to Belcoo opened in 1879, and reached Manorhamilton in 1880. Problems in raising capital led in 1880 to a return to parliament for an extension of the time allowed to build the line and powers to raise more funds to complete the works. The company already had a loan of £100,000 from the Board of Works, and when SL&NCR trains began running through to Sligo in 1882, as evidence of the company's impoverished state, all its rolling stock was hired from one of its shareholders. In 1890 it was put into receivership and the Board of Works threatened to sell it to the MGWR and GNR. The SL&NCR managed to avoid this fate and, as we shall see later, was to be one of the last independent Irish railway companies.

Having achieved its original objective with the opening of the line to Armagh in 1848, the Ulster Railway doggedly pursued the course set out in its original prospectus of 1835 and headed west. The first extension was to Monaghan, opened in May 1858, and then to Clones in 1863, where it made a junction

with the D&E. To continue the line to Cavan the Clones and Cavan Extension Railway was established, under the wing of the D&E but mainly financed by contributions from the UR, D&BJR and D&D. At Cavan the line made a junction with the MGWR, which had reached the town from the south in 1856. The UR also backed the building of a line from Portadown to Dungannon and Omagh, which opened to Dungannon in 1858 and Omagh in 1861. The one branch off this line, from Dungannon to Cookstown, opened in 1879. At Omagh a junction was made with the L&E line from Derry, providing a second route between Belfast and Londonderry.

Going back to the Dublin to Belfast main line, when we left the Newry and Enniskillen Railway in the previous chapter it had taken the company eight years to scrape up enough funds to build the four miles from Newry to a junction with the D&BJR at Goraghwood. Its plan to reach Enniskillen via Armagh and Clones, being a roundabout route over difficult terrain, was clearly never going to be fulfilled. The powers for the Enniskillen part of its route lapsed, and this was eventually built by the D&E. In 1857 the company changed its name to the Newry and Armagh and embarked on an eighteen-mile line from Goraghwood to join the UR. This route was characterised by steep banks and required two tunnels, of which the 1,759-yard Lisummon Tunnel, between Goraghwood and Markethill, was the longest railway tunnel in Ireland. The line to Armagh finally opened in 1864.

included the 135-yard long Kilpatrick tunnel, the first in Ireland to be used by passenger trains. Services on the final section to Cork Albert Quay station, which included another tunnel, the much longer 900-yard Goggins Hill tunnel, and the lofty Chetwynd Viaduct, 90 feet high and consisting of four 110-feet-long iron spans, commenced in December 1851.

The first addition to the C&B system was a branch promoted by a separate company, the Cork and Kinsale Junction Railway, which in 1863 opened its eleven-mile long line to the fishing port of Kinsale on the south coast, diverging from the Bandon line at Kinsale Junction. The main line was also gradually extended west from Bandon. The West Cork Railway opened a line eighteen miles long from Bandon to Dunmanway in 1866. Another independent company, the Ilen Valley Railway, further extended this line to Skibbereen in 1877. The Cork, Blackrock and Passage Railway, authorised in 1846, opened its short line of six and a half miles from a terminus at Victoria Road to Passage in June 1850.

There was one other railway company in County Cork, the Cork and Macroom Direct Railway, which was authorised in 1861 to build a line from Cork to the small market town of Macroom, twenty-four miles to the west of the city. The line opened in 1866, and at first its trains shared the C&B station at Albert Quay, joining C&B metals at Ballyphehane Junction, a mile out from the terminus. The Bandon company was paid £2,000 per year for the use of their facilities. Disputes between the two companies soon arose, with the C&MDR believing it was paying too much

Opening of the C&MDR, 12 May 1866 (above).

C&MDR 0–6–2T locomotive No. 5 (below).

for the use of the C&B's facilities, and the C&B being of the opinion that the Macroom company was not paying enough. They were unable to come to an equitable agreement, the C&B declining arbitration offered by the Board of Trade. In 1877 the C&MDR sought powers to build its own line into the city, and in 1879 opened a terminus at Capwell, some distance from the city centre. The junction at Ballyphehane was severed, and the Macroom line continued in splendid isolation until a connection with the Bandon line was re-established during the First World War. The lack of any kind of planning or overall strategy resulted in Cork city having, by 1879, no fewer than five separate railway stations, four of them termini, only two of which were linked to each other.

North of Cork, the Killarney Junction Railway was authorised in 1846 to build a line from Mallow to Killarney, a popular tourist destination. The KJR had the strong backing of the GS&WR,

TYPE No 35322

The Cork, Blackrock and Passage Railway, essentially a suburban commuter service, opened as a broad-gauge line in 1850 and was converted to 3ft gauge in 1900. In this scene from about 1914, painted by Sean Bolan, 2–4–2T No. 5 passes Cork Marina.

Sir John Macneill

In the person of Sir John Macneill, Ireland produced an outstanding railway engineer who deserves to be considered among the first rank. He is not perhaps of the same stature as the likes of the Stephensons, Locke and Brunel, but he is not far behind them.

Macneill was born near Dundalk in 1793 and followed his father into military service. On leaving the ranks as a lieutenant he became a road surveyor working for the turnpike trusts who maintained the sections of the Dublin to Belfast road between Newry, Dundalk and Dunleer. During a trip to England in the 1820s he met the great engineer Thomas Telford. He was building the new road from London to Holyhead at the time, and Macneill was employed as assistant engineer on the sections of the road between London and Shrewsbury. He worked with Telford for over ten years on a variety of road and canal projects. Ironically, for a man who was to find fame as a railway engineer, in the early 1830s he was a strong advocate of steam road traction, being employed by the London and Birmingham Steam Carriage Company in 1832 and later in 1835 by the London, Holyhead and Liverpool Steam Coach and Road Company.

When Thomas Drummond, the Under Secretary of State for Ireland, set up a commission to report on a railway network for Ireland in 1838, Macneill surveyed the northern part of the country, and when railway construction began in the 1840s his most significant contribution was in the building of most of the railway from Dublin to Belfast. He was the engineer for the Dublin and Drogheda Railway and later for the Dublin and Belfast Junction company. In May 1844, Macneill was knighted by the Lord Lieutenant of Ireland at the official opening of the D&D. Between 1840 and his last Irish commission, as engineer on the first sections of the Londonderry and Lough Swilly Railway in the 1860s, he was responsible for many miles of railway in his native land. He was also the engineer for railway schemes in England and Scotland and on overseas railway projects in countries such as Belgium and France and the Euphrates Valley Railway in the Middle East. He also supervised the construction of the Belfast Waterworks in the 1840s and its expansion in the 1860s, and prepared plans for a water supply system for Jerusalem in 1865.

Macneill's greatest contribution to his native land lies in two very specific areas. The first of these was his role in the teaching of engineering in Ireland. He was appointed as the first professor of civil engineering at Trinity College in Dublin in 1842, a position he held for ten years. The first engineering graduate from Trinity was James Barton, whose schemes included the building of the port of Greenore. Macneill's other legacy was the major part he played in determining the gauge used on the Irish railway system. His recommendation of a gauge of 5ft 2in to the directors of the D&D was only slightly modified by the Board of Trade, who had the final word on the most significant of all Irish railway measurements.

ultimately lost £20,000 on the project. Such was his prestige, at this time he entertained Queen Victoria at his house in south Dublin. In order to encourage visitors from the north to attend, a temporary timber viaduct was built over the Boyne, opening on 22 June 1853, which for the first time allowed railway passengers an uninterrupted journey between Belfast and Dublin. The timber structure was later replaced by a lattice girder viaduct which opened in April 1855.

By the 1860s, Dargan had moved on from being a railway builder to become a railway executive and manager as chairman of the Dublin, Wicklow and Wexford Railway. In 1866 he was seriously injured by a fall from his horse. Unable to work following the accident, he suffered a great downturn in his finances. Neither his health nor his business ever recovered from the effects of the accident. He died at his house in Fitzwilliam Square East in Dublin on 7 February 1867 and was buried at Glasnevin cemetery in the city.

Dargan's monument is the many miles of railway which he constructed that are still in use throughout Ireland to this day. He is also appropriately commemorated in two bridges in Belfast and Dublin built in the last two decades. The first of these, the Dargan Bridge over the River Lagan in Belfast, was opened in 1994 and provides a link between the former B&NCR routes from Londonderry and Larne and the rest of the network at Belfast Central station. The second, the William Dargan Bridge

at Dundrum in south Dublin, carries the Luas tramway across a busy road intersection. This part of the Luas system runs on the trackbed of the former Dublin and South Eastern Railway's line from Bray to Harcourt Street station in Dublin, which closed in 1958. Appropriately, this was one of the many lines constructed by Dargan during the course of his illustrious career.

The strong lines of the Dargan Bridge at Dundrum (Infomatique).

advantage of putting the MGWR in a position to repel invasion from the south in the form of the GJR or another GS&WR satellite, and could be extended from Longford towards Sligo. The section from Mullingar to Longford opened in 1855, and services commenced on the Cavan line in July 1856. Next the Midland finally took steps to build a line from Longford to Sligo. The Sligo Extension Act of 1857 allowed the company to raise an extra £580,000 to build the fifty-eight-mile long route. The MGWR's second main line opened in December 1862.

In addition to being an attack on MGWR activities, the GS&WR-sponsored Grand Junction Company also reflected a growing demand for railways to serve County Mayo. Lord Lucan, a major landowner in the area, chaired a meeting at Castlebar to discuss railway expansion in Mayo in October 1852. Fatally for many of the soldiers of the Light Brigade which he commanded, he put his railway activities on hold to preside, in October 1854, over perhaps the greatest British military disaster of the nineteenth century, when he ordered his regiment to charge Russian gun emplacements in the Crimea. Back in Ireland in 1855, his name appeared, along with that of John Ennis of the MGWR, on the provisional committee of the North Western Railway of Ireland, which planned to build a line to Castlebar. This scheme was rejected by parliament in 1856, but its successor, the Great Northern and Western, again with Lucan at the helm, was authorised in 1857 to raise £240,000 to build lines from Athlone to Castlebar, Westport and Ballina, lines which the Midland was to work. The railway opened in stages, reaching Castlerea in 1861, Claremorris and Castlebar in 1862, and Westport in 1866. Ballina had to wait until 1873 when the branch from Manulla Junction reached the town.

In 1857 parliament finally authorised the GS&WR to complete its long-desired branch to Athlone. The

Lord Lucan, 3rd Earl, in a Spy cartoon from *Vanity Fair*.

act, however, stated that the GS&WR line was not to cross the Shannon, so it built its station at Athlone to the east of the river. Peace eventually prevailed between the two companies in 1860, when they agreed to allow two distinguished English railway managers to act as arbitrators. The result was a line of demarcation defining their respective spheres of influence, which ran roughly across the centre of Ireland from Dublin to Athlone, and down the Shannon to its estuary. The MGWR was to stay to the north of this and the GS&WR to the south and southeast, each being prohibited from promoting lines or funding satellite companies in each other's territories. By and large both companies stuck to the agreement.

The Midland was a geographically compact system, and few branches were built between 1850 and 1880. The first, to the west of Dublin, was the Dublin and Meath Railway, which received royal assent in 1858 to build a line from a junction with the MGWR near Clonsilla to Navan, with a branch from Kilmessan Junction to Athboy. The line, which was worked by the MGWR, opened to Navan in 1862, the branch to Trim and Athboy following in 1864. In 1869 the line was extended to make a junction with the Dublin and Drogheda line which had reached Navan in 1850. The D&D was itself extended to meet the D&M line at Navan Junction. In 1864 a separate company, the Navan and Kingscourt, was empowered to build a line from what became Navan Junction to Kingscourt in County Cavan, which was finally reached in 1875.

The next branch line after Clonsilla was that to Edenderry, which left the main line at Nesbitt Junction, just west of Enfield, twenty-eight miles from Dublin. This served the small market town of Edenderry and opened in April 1877. The proposal to build a line to the town was floundering on the common problem of raising the capital, in this case over £20,000, but the impasse was resolved through the generosity of a local landowner, a Miss Nesbitt, who offered £10,000 towards the cost of the line. In grateful thanks for her largesse the junction was named after her. The only other MGWR branch line built in this period was not encountered until Kilfree Junction in County Sligo was reached, 112 miles from Dublin, from where a line served the small County Roscommon town of Ballaghaderreen.

The development of the east coast line was driven by Brunel's Great Western Railway which, through its subsidiary the South Wales Railway, was looking to establish a port in west Wales linked to a new port south of Wexford in order to take a share of the Irish Sea traffic. In order to link this proposed new Irish terminal with Dublin, the GWR backed the Waterford, Wexford, Wicklow and Dublin Railway. Two lines already existed from Bray to Dublin; in 1855 the original Dublin to Kingstown line was regauged to 5ft 3in, and the extension to Dalkey was converted from atmospheric to conventional working, allowing through running from Dublin to Bray along the coastal route. Originally opened to a station at Harcourt Road, the line was soon extended to a final terminus at Harcourt Street, still some distance from the centre of the city. When reality caught up with the WWW&D, and the great scheme for the new port and lines to Wexford and Waterford was officially dropped in an act of 1851, the company reconstituted itself as the Dublin and Wicklow Railway and focused on that more modest objective, which it reached in 1855.

In time the line from Wicklow was extended down the east coast. In 1859 the company changed its name

Bray station on an 1899 postcard.

to the Dublin, Wicklow and Wexford, reflecting its next intended destination. Enniscorthy was reached in 1863 and Wexford in 1872, over twenty years behind schedule. There were two branches along the ninety-mile line. The first, just a quarter of a mile long, opened in 1859, linking the main line to the pier at Kingstown and allowing trains to connect with steamers from Holyhead. The other branch, opened in 1865, was sixteen miles long, from Woodenbridge Junction to Shillelagh.

The one other development in the south-east was the incorporation in 1863 of the Waterford and Wexford Railway to build a line linking those towns and, harking back to Brunel and the GWR, a branch to Greenore where a pier was to be constructed. Greenore later came to be known as Rosslare. Construction proceeded at snail's pace, and the only parts of the scheme to be completed were the pier and a line linking Rosslare to the DW&W along the quays at Wexford, which opened in 1882. The line was worked by the DW&W, but receipts were so poor that the service was suspended in 1889. The real significance of this line would not be realised until the next century.

The progress made by the Waterford and Limerick Railway after the first part of its line opened to Limerick Junction and Tipperary in 1848 was more measured. With the aid of a loan of £120,000 from the Public Works Loan Commissioners, Clonmel was reached in 1852, and trains began to run to a station at Newrath, on the western outskirts of Waterford, in September 1854. W&L trains did not reach the site of the present Waterford station until 1864. The year before the W&L reached Newrath the Waterford and Kilkenny gave the city a link to Dublin via Kilkenny. An extension of the GS&WR branch to Carlow was opened to Kilkenny in 1850 by the Irish South Eastern Railway, a GS&WR satellite. The ISER was formally taken over by the GS&WR in 1863. A further line

A share certificate for the Waterford and Limerick Railway.

was built from Kilkenny in the 1860s, a route north to Maryborough via Abbeyleix. Built by the Kilkenny Junction Railway, this opened in 1867.

Back in Waterford, the seven-mile long Waterford and Tramore Railway also opened for business. This line was unique in several ways: it was very prosperous, in its early years paying dividends of over 7 per cent, and for its entire existence it remained physically isolated from the rest of the Irish railway network. The W&T had no intermediate stations or passing places, and its terminus, Waterford Manor, was over a mile away from the main station in the city.

Before 1900 there was only one branch off the entire Limerick to Waterford route, from Clonmel to Thurles. This was originally promoted as long ago as 1846, but was revived in 1865 by the impressively-titled Southern Railway. The attraction of this twenty-five-mile line was that it should have offered a faster route from Clonmel to Dublin than the trek via Limerick Junction, but the usual catalogue of financial difficulties plagued the company, which in the end needed substantial loans from the Public Works Loan Commissioners to complete the construction works. The line opened as far as Fethard in 1879, and to a junction with the GS&WR main line at Thurles in July 1880. The SR was worked from the outset by the W&L, but by 1884 it was insolvent and ownership passed to the Board of Works, though the W&L continued to provide the service.

The main activities of the W&L were centred on Limerick. By the time it had reached its greatest extent, the W&L was the fourth largest railway in Ireland. However, its main line from Limerick to Waterford was only seventy-seven miles long; most of its growth came from absorbing smaller concerns or working their routes. The lines which spread southwest from Limerick took nearly thirty years to reach Tralee in 1880. The first part of this line, from Limerick to Ballingrane, was opened in 1856 by the Limerick and Foynes Railway; Foynes was reached two years later. This line was extended ten miles to Newcastle West in 1867 by a separate company, the Rathkeale and Newcastle Junction, which left Ballingrane as the junction for the port of Foynes on the Shannon estuary. Both lines were worked by the W&L.

Yet another company, the Limerick and North Kerry, was authorised in 1873 to build a line forty-two and a half miles long from Newcastle to Tralee. The W&L provided £25,000 of the company's £260,000 capital and worked the line when it opened. The North Kerry line, as it came to be known, was a difficult one to construct. L&NK tracks did not make an end-on junction with the existing line at Newcastle West, so the locomotives of through trains had to run round their stock before continuing. From Newcastle West to Barnagh the line climbed on gradients as steep as 1 in 61. The 110-yard long tunnel at Barnagh was the only one on the entire W&L system, and just beyond this, at a summit of 630ft above sea level, the highest point on any Irish standard gauge railway was reached.

The W&L also expanded north from Limerick, taking its trains into Kerry. The Limerick and Ennis Railway was authorised in 1853, but by 1856 the company had run out of funds. In 1857 the Public

Works Loan Commissioners came to the rescue with a loan of £40,000, and the line opened in 1859. From the outset it was worked by the W&L, and was absorbed by that company in 1874.

As the Ennis line was stuttering towards completion, a new company, the Athenry and Ennis Junction Railway, was incorporated to continue the route north to make a junction at Athenry with the MGWR's Galway to Dublin line. Incorporated in 1860, it did not open its thirty-six-mile long line until 1869, once again with help from the Public Works Loan Commissioners. The A&EJR was also worked by the W&L, into which it was eventually absorbed. North from Athenry a line had been opened to Tuam by the Athenry and Tuam Railway in 1860. This was worked initially by the MGWR but later by the W&L, which used it as a springboard for further expansion to the north.

The thirty years from 1850 saw an astonishing growth in the extent of the Irish railway network. At the start of the 1850s there were some 800 miles of railway in Ireland. By 1880 this had risen to 2,400 miles of standard gauge track. Railways now served virtually all the country's major towns and cities, and also penetrated many rural districts. Yet many of the companies were on the very margins of profitability, and a large number had needed substantial Treasury loans to complete their lines. Even a company like the Belfast and County Down, which had originally been profitable, needed assistance to keep afloat in the difficult financial climate of the 1860s.

Despite this, and the fact that investment in many Irish railway schemes had proved to be far from profitable, there were still many miles to be built before the national network reached its greatest extent. The next part of our story deals with this last great spurt of railway building, and takes us into the era when the railways of Ireland reached the height of their importance.

Chapter 4

THE GOLDEN AGE OF

IRELAND'S RAILWAYS, 1880–1914

The golden age for the railways of Ireland came in the three and a half decades between 1880 and the start of the First World War in August 1914. In terms of route mileage the national network reached its greatest extent in these years, and a new, extensive and complementary network of narrow gauge tracks was also laid down in these decades. In this period the railways had a virtual monopoly of the available traffic, but despite this the receipts generated by many lines were barely enough to cover their running costs. Many of the new lines were subsidised in one way or another by local or national government, and would not have been built without this support. Even though the railways were at the height of their influence in the years covered by this chapter, there were underlying structural problems which only became fully apparent after 1914.

By the end of the 1870s there were about 2,400 route miles of railway in Ireland. Most of the major towns were connected to the network, but there were still many districts with no access to a railway. Finding the capital to build lines in Ireland was never easy, especially in the more remote parts of the country, and the existing network was probably about as large

as conventional methods of railway promotion could deliver. After the financial crisis of the mid-1860s, precipitated by the collapse of the London bank Overend and Guerney, railway construction slowed down considerably and never really recovered.

The government, through the Board of Works, had been providing loans to help railway construction since the 1830s, but these were commercial transactions on which interest had to be paid, and the loans ultimately had to be discharged. Several companies, such as the Bagenalstown and Wexford and the Letterkenny Railway, were put out of business by the Board of Works when they failed to meet their commitments. Given the choice of buying shares in a line in a populous part of Britain, maybe one rich in mineral wealth, and one in a remote part of Ireland where the population had been on the decline since the 1850s, an investor would scarcely rush to invest in the Irish scheme. If the demand for additional railways was to be met, something else had to be tried.

The first of these initiatives was the Tramways Act of 1883, which attempted to provide a stimulus to railway construction in disadvantaged areas by allowing the promoters of a line to approach a county's Grand Jury to seek financial support for their scheme. The Grand Juries, unelected bodies usually dominated

Belfast and County Down Railway 4–4–2T No. 3 passing Downpatrick Cathedral, 1905, a painting by Jack Hill.

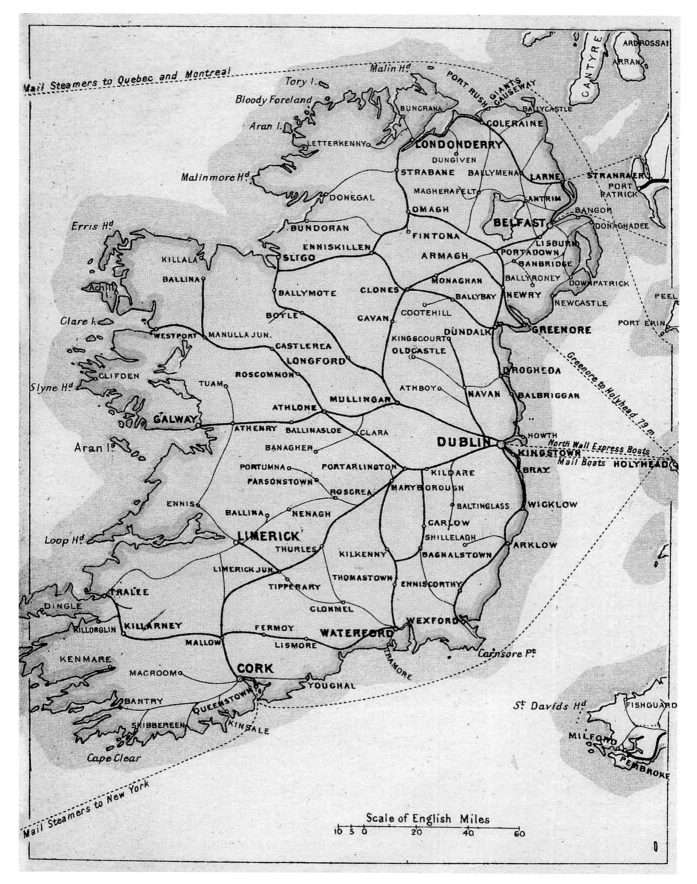

by landowners, dated back to the time of Charles I, and were replaced by County and District councils only in 1898. They were responsible for the administration of a county and for setting the county rate.

Each county was subdivided into districts or baronies, which gave rise to an instrument associated with many of the railways promoted and built under the terms of the Tramways Act – the baronial guarantee. Under the Act, if a railway scheme met the approval of the Grand Jury it could undertake to guarantee the interest on the capital employed to build the line, and to identify the baronies benefiting from the building of the route that were to fund it. The Act made no mention of what gauge should be used, but in the General Tramways Order issued by the Lord Lieutenant the same year the gauge of 'tramways' was specified as three feet. This made promoters easier to find, since narrow gauge lines were much cheaper to construct than broad gauge ones, though baronial guarantees were later allowed to be used to support 5ft 3in gauge lines.

Interest on the capital employed in railway construction was guaranteed at up to 5 per cent. Suddenly the promotion of a line in a sleepy backwater in Ireland was transformed from being a highly risky enterprise into a gilt-edged investment. In 1882 twenty-three of the forty Irish railway companies included in the Board of Trade returns paid no dividends at all on their ordinary capital, while nine paid under 4 per cent, and only eight exceeded that amount.

While the Tramways Act delivered many miles of railway, there was an inherent flaw in the process. While the Act provided financial incentives in the form of baronial guarantees, it set no guidelines as to who were fit and proper persons to promote and build

A map of 1887, showing all the Irish railways built up to that date. There are still many gaps which would later be filled, notably down the west coast in Donegal, Mayo, Galway, Clare and Kerry.

a railway. The lines supported under this scheme were often seen as being of most benefit to the landowners whose interests dominated the Grand Juries, whilst the cost of the baronial guarantees had to be met by the ordinary ratepayers in the districts served by the lines. This led to monumental rows over the management of lines in several parts of Ireland. An unwisely promoted or badly run railway, rather than being a boon to a district, could become a serious financial burden for the unfortunate ratepayers.

The first 3ft gauge lines in Ireland opened in County Antrim between 1872 and 1880. Two based at Ballymena were promoted to transport iron ore from the Antrim Glens to Larne for export. A third linked the seaside town of Ballycastle to the B&NCR at Ballymoney. These were all promoted without the aid of baronial guarantees. A further short 3ft steam tramway which linked the County Derry seaside town of Portstewart to its distant station on the branch from Coleraine to Portrush opened in 1882.

The next twenty-five years saw narrow gauge lines built in many parts of Ireland, from Donegal to Cork and Kerry. Two served Cork city – the Cork, Blackrock and Passage Railway, a busy commuter line, and the Cork and Muskerry, which served rural areas to the northwest of the city. West Cork had the Schull and Skibbereen Tramway, and Kerry the Tralee and Dingle Railway, consisting of a thirty-two-mile-long main line from Tralee to Dingle and a short six-mile branch from Camp (later renamed Castlegregory Junction) to Castlegregory. From Dingle station a short branch continued to the harbour, and at Tralee there were interchange sidings with the broad gauge in the GS&WR yard, though passengers had to walk several hundred yards between the town's broad and narrow gauge stations.

Another lengthy affair was the West Clare Railway, forty-eight miles long from Ennis to Kilkee and a mile less to Kilrush via a branch from Moyasta Junction. Further north was the Cavan and Leitrim Railway.

Guard Michael Talty's Brush with Fame

Railways need a lot of manpower to keep them running, and some women power as well, to be fair to the girls, though the women were often left to run the buffets or open the gates at level crossings. Not for them the glamour of life on the footplate. As late as the 1950s, it was reckoned that for every mile of railway open in the Irish Republic six people were employed. They remained largely anonymous, rarely appearing even in archive photographs. This, however, is the story of one railwayman who was thrust into the spotlight in the most singular fashion and whose name will live as long as the song in which he features is heard.

William Percy French was born in County Roscommon in 1854. He trained as an engineer at Trinity College Dublin but found fame as a composer and performer of comic songs mainly about life in rural Ireland, many of which are still sung today. On Monday 10 August 1896, French left the Broadstone in Dublin to travel to Kilkee in County Clare to fulfil an engagement that evening at Moore's Concert Hall. He made the connection

Percy French in 1900.

West Clare locomotive No. 3c at Ennis, 1900 (left).

Schoolgirls on the way to school in Ennis on the West Clare in 1937 (opposite).

off the broad gauge at Ennis onto the 3ft gauge West Clare Railway's 12.40pm train to Kilkee. All went well as far as Miltown Malbay where the locomotive, No. 8 *Lisdoonvarna*, was declared a failure by its driver. Vegetation had somehow got into the water tanks, blocking the injectors which fed the water into the boiler and leaving the crew no option but to drop the fire, thus rendering the locomotive a failure. While the railway staff acted promptly to try and get a relief engine for the Kilkee train, there was at that time a sixteen-mile single track section from Miltown Malbay south to Moyasta Junction, with no crossing place in between. This long single track section slowed the arrival of the replacement engine, No. 4 *Besborough*.

On the footplate of that engine, there travelled a new guard for the delayed train, one Michael Talty, on a duty that would bring him immortality, though he was not to know it at the time. The train carrying Percy French eventually arrived at Kilkee at 8.00pm, but when he reached the hall he found his audience had largely dispersed and, while he did perform, it was to a very poor house. Matters might have rested there, but Percy French sued the company for loss of earnings of £10. Had the directors of the company any sense, they would have settled there and then with the entertainer, but they did not and the case came to court. French, a renowned humourist, gave a fine performance in the witness box in a case which was well reported and obviously gave him more than £10's worth of free publicity. The judge embraced the spirit of the proceedings and awarded French costs and damages of £10.

In a hole, but apparently determined to carry on digging, the company appealed the decision and, three months later, when their appeal was heard, they lost again. At the second hearing it became apparent that for the recalcitrant directors of the company a further penalty was in the offing when Percy French shared with the court a few lines from a comic song he was writing about what he called 'the wild West Clare'. The song, commonly known as *Are Ye Right There Michael?*, was later published and is still performed. It secured for the West Clare Railway Company, and for Michael Talty in particular, a unique kind of fame. In homage to its composer and to the line it made famous or infamous, we can do no more than give you all the stanzas of one of the most amusing songs ever written about a railway.

Are Ye Right There, Michael?

You may talk of Columbus's sailing
Across the Atlantical sea,
But he never tried to go railing
From Ennis as far as Kilkee.
You run for the train in the morning,
The excursion train starting at eight.
You're there when the guard gives the warning,
And there for an hour you'll wait.

And while you're waiting in the train,
You'll hear the guard sing this refrain:
Are ye right there, Michael, are ye right?
Do you think that we'll be home before the night?
Ye've been so long in startin',
That ye couldn't say for certain
Still ye might now, Michael,
So ye might!

They find out where the engine's been hiding,
And it drags you to sweet Corofin;
Says the guard: Back her down on the siding,
There's a goods from Kilrush comin' in.
Perhaps it comes in two hours,
Perhaps it breaks down on the way;
If it does, says the guard, be the powers,
We're here for the rest of the day!

And while you sit and curse your luck,
The train backs down into a truck.
Are ye right there, Michael, are ye right?
Have ye got the parcel there for Mrs. White?
Ye haven't, oh begorra,
Say it's comin' down tomorra
And well it might now, Michael,
So it might!

At Lahinch the sea shines like a jewel,
With joy you are ready to shout,
When the stoker cries out: There's no fuel,
And the fire is teetotally out.
But hand up that bit of a log there
I'll soon have ye out of the fix;
There's fine clamp of turf in the bog there.
And the rest can go gatherin' sticks.

And while you're breakin' bits off trees,
You hear some wise remarks like these:
Are ye right there, Michael? Are ye right?
Do ye think that you can get the fire to light?
Oh, an hour you'll require,
For the turf it might be drier,
Well it might now, Michael,
So it might!

Kilkee! Oh, ye'll never get near it,
You're in luck if the train brings you back.
For the permanent way is so queer, it
Spends most of its time off the track.
Uphill the oul' engine is climbing,
As the passengers push with a will.
You're in luck when you reach Ennistimon,
For all the way home is downhill.

And as you're wobbling through the dark,
You'll hear someone make this remark:
Are ye right there, Michael? Are ye right?
Do you think that we'll be there before it's light?
Oh, it's all depending whether,
The oul' engine holds together,
But it might now, Michael,
So it might!

West Clare Railway, No. 1 *Kilrush* and No. 5 *Slieve Callan* at Moyasta Junction, 1920, a painting by Jack Hill.

Most of the burden of guaranteeing the 5 per cent interest on the £190,585 it cost to build fell on the ratepayers of County Leitrim, with a smaller contribution from County Cavan through which the northern part of the line passed. The main line ran from a junction with the MGWR's Dublin to Sligo line at Dromod north to Belturbet, where it shared a station with a GNR branch from Ballyhaise on the Cavan to Clones line. From Ballinamore, the hub of the line and the site of its workshops, a branch went to Arigna in County Roscommon whose coal mines were connected to the railway in 1920. Happily for Roscommon ratepayers, their Grand Jury declined to get involved in backing the scheme. Some rancorous rows flared after the Grand Juries were replaced by elected County Councils in 1898. On the C&L the board quickly divided into two opposing camps, with distinct political and religious affiliations. In 1902 the original directors managed to rig the composition of the board to leave the ratepayers'

representatives in a permanent minority, creating friction that continued for many years.

The greatest concentration of narrow gauge lines was in Ulster, and a varied lot they were. The Clogher Valley Tramway (the name was changed to Railway in 1894) would almost certainly never have been built without the benefit of baronial guarantees. The capital needed to construct the thirty-seven-mile-long line from Tynan to Maguiresbridge was £150,000, which the Grand Juries of Tyrone and Fermanagh agreed to guarantee in March 1884. The CVR was a roadside tramway for most of its route, though at Fivemiletown trains ran down the middle of the main street. The line was far from a financial success. It failed to show an operating profit in its first seven years, a pattern which was followed throughout most of its existence.

Clogher Valley Railway No. 2 and No. 3 haul a Fairday Special through Fivemiletown in the early 1930s, a painting by Victor Welch.

Even in its most prosperous year, 1904, receipts were only £791 more than its working expenses. In that year alone, the guaranteed dividends paid to shareholders cost the ratepayers £5,375. County Tyrone also had another steam tramway, the less ambitious Castlederg and Victoria Bridge Tramway, which ran the seven miles from the small market town of Castlederg to the GNR station at Victoria Bridge on the line from Derry to Portadown.

The usual image of Irish narrow gauge working is of venerable steam locomotives bouncing along roadside tramways. Two of Ulster's 3ft gauge lines, however, were at the cutting edge of a new technology. When they were opened in the 1880s they were powered by new-fangled electricity.

From the middle of the nineteenth century, the spinning of flax and the production of linen became a major industry in Ulster. Some of the first mills were built at Bessbrook, near Newry in County Armagh. The need to provide transport from Newry for both materials and workers led to the building of a three-mile-long 3ft gauge electric tramway, which opened on 1 October 1885. Power was provided by a hydro-electric power station at Millvale, near Bessbrook, and the line was constructed by Edward Hopkinson, a pioneer of electric traction. 245 volts DC was supplied

to the cars from a third rail between the tracks. The line passed under the Craigmore Viaduct on the GNR's Dublin to Belfast main line, and part of its trackbed can still be seen from trains passing overhead.

Ulster's other electric railway was the Giant's Causeway, Portrush and Bush Valley Railway and Tramway Company. This little tramway, less than ten miles long and running along one of the most beautiful stretches of coastline in Ireland, was at the cutting edge of science in the 1880s. Different methods of delivering current to the line were explored. The original idea was to use a two-rail system, but especially in wet weather too much current was lost. The directors settled on running the current through a third or conductor rail located on the coastal side of the line, away from the public road. Power was provided by a hydro-electric station at Walkmills near Bushmills. Construction began in 1881 from the Bushmills end and the line was inspected and approved by the Board of Trade in January 1883, having cost £21,000 to build. The use of the third rail was not permitted at the extremities of the line, where it ran through the streets of Bushmills and Portrush to reach its termini. On these sections, and for goods traffic, steam locomotives were used. The line was extended to the Giant's Causeway, then as now one of Ireland's main tourist attractions, in July 1887.

Ireland's two largest narrow gauge systems were in County Donegal, and both began life as broad gauge lines. The first to get under way was the Londonderry

Tooban Junction signal box in the 1920s (J. W. F. Scrimgeour)

and Lough Swilly Railway, which was incorporated in the early 1850s to build a line from the city of Derry to a pier at Farland Point on the shores of Lough Swilly. Construction did not start until 1860, and it was 1863 before the first train ran to Farland Point, from where boats served the small communities around the shores of the Lough. In 1861 an Act authorised the L&LSR to extend its line along the eastern shore of Lough Swilly to Buncrana. This route left the existing line at a remote spot which in the 1920s became known as Tooban Junction, and there was another short branch to a pier at Fahan, which opened in September 1864. The line from the junction to Farland Point closed in 1866 after one of the shortest innings in the entire history of Ireland's railways. Meanwhile, the Letterkenny Railway Company had been attempting since 1860 to build a railway to that town. The LR obtained a new Act in 1880 authorising a narrow gauge railway, which also gave the L&LSR the power to regauge their existing line. With the aid of a loan of £85,000 from the Board of Works, the line from Letterkenny to Tooban Junction opened in June 1883. The LR was worked from the outset by the L&LSR, which converted its existing line from Derry to Buncrana to 3ft gauge in the spring of 1885.

The first component of Donegal's other narrow gauge system was authorised in 1860. The Finn Valley Railway obtained powers to build a line fourteen miles long from Strabane to the twin towns of Ballybofey and Stranorlar. When it opened in August 1863 the line was worked by the INWR on behalf of the FVR. Traffic never lived up to the levels expected, and a solution was proposed in an extension from Stranorlar to Donegal Town. A separate company, the West Donegal Railway, was formed with the backing of the FVR board. In 1879 the WDR was authorised to raise £150,000 to build the 3ft gauge line through the Barnsmore Gap in the Blue Stack Mountains. Difficulties in raising the capital soon emerged, and by 1881 it was clear that there was not enough money to complete the line to Donegal Town. Building stalled at Druminin, near Lough Eske, four miles from the intended destination. When services began in 1882 trains went no further than Druminin, a situation which continued until the gap was eventually closed in 1889.

Traditional methods of railway promotion had clearly not been a great success in delivering a railway network to County Donegal, yet the demand for more railways remained. Politics now entered the equation, and railway building became part of an ambitious and complex political and economic strategy which had at

Londonderry and Lough Swilly Railway 4–8–0 No. 12 on the Burtonport line, coping with rough terrain and severe weather conditions. Only two of these locomotives were ever built; they had the distinction of being the only narrow-gauge tender engines in Ireland and the only tender locomotives with this wheel arrangement ever used in the British Isles. The painting is by Sean Bolan.

Sean Bolan '82

The Intriguing Lartigue

Unquestionably the strangest railway which ever operated, not just in Ireland, but in the whole of the British Isles, was that which ran from Listowel to Ballybunion in County Kerry from 1888 to 1924.

Ballybunion is an agreeable small seaside town in the north of the county. Similar towns from Portrush to Tramore had prospered with the coming of the railway, so it is not surprising that the burghers of Ballybunion wanted to sip from this tourist honeypot. Several schemes for both broad gauge lines and narrow gauge tramways linking the town to the nearby north Kerry line were promoted in the 1880s without success. However, unknown to its citizens, the solution to Ballybunion's transport problems was already in existence. It had been devised by one Charles François Marie-Thérèse Lartigue, a French engineer working in his country's colonies in North Africa, who had been thinking about ways of designing a cheap method for constructing railways in remote locations.

Lartigue had observed the heavy loads which camels could carry through the desert on pallets hung from their humps, which inspired him to think about a monorail. Lartigue's system involved a running rail which was carried at the top of 'A'-shaped metal trestles whose legs were fixed at the bottom onto wood or metal sleepers. There were light rails about a foot above the sleepers fixed to the outside of the uprights of the 'A' frames to stabilise the rolling stock. The trains ran on vertical double-flanged rails which bore all the weight. Rolling stock also had horizontal double-flanged wheels which ran on the outside rails.

The Lartigue system was first used in North Africa in connection with the production of esparto grass, used in paper making. Transport was by wagons hauled by mules. The track was light and could easily be dismantled and erected elsewhere. The road which brought the Lartigue railway from the deserts of North Africa to the coast of north Kerry was routed through the centre of London. In the 1880s, in what today is one of the most exclusive parts of the city, between Victoria Street and Birdcage Walk, was a piece of waste ground called Tothill Fields. In 1886, a demonstration line was built

there to show off the Lartigue monorail. This showed all the advantages of the system – steep grades, sharp curves and turntables to enable stock to switch tracks. The Lartigue Company wanted a permanent line to demonstrate the system and the people of Ballybunion wanted a railway.

These two aspirations came together and a company was formed to build a monorail from Ballybunion to meet the north Kerry line at Listowel. The line was built by the company at a cost of £33,000. Construction began in late 1887 and the line was opened in March of the following year. Three 0–3–0 tender engines were supplied by the Hunslet Engine Company of Leeds to work the line. The service was similar to that offered on many minor Irish lines, with three trains a day and additional services in summer.

The Lartigue was completely different from a conventional railway. For example, the passenger coaches, slung from the monorail, had longitudinal seats, which meant that the passengers' heads were next to the running rail. This must have made travel on the trains incredibly noisy. Loadings on either side of the train had to be equalised, which was not so much a problem with passengers, but if livestock were being transported, a cow on one side of the wagon would have to be balanced by a couple of sheep or pigs on the other.

However, the most insane feature of the railway was the belief on the part of the directors

Changing points at Ballybunion on the Listowel and Ballybunion Railway, 1910 (above).

The opening of the Listowel and Ballybunion Railway in 1888, a contemporary engraving (opposite).

of the Lartigue company that decision makers, captains of industry and military men from the great European colonial empires would visit County Kerry to view this wonderful new advance in light railway technology. Nobody came of course, and though the company was in receivership in 1897 the railway struggled on. Its only hope was that it could make enough revenue from visitors during the summer months to sustain it through the winter when traffic was sparse. Its most prosperous year was 1913, when it made a surplus of £875. Traffic declined during the First World War and the monorail suffered some malicious damage during the Civil War. When the railways of the twenty-six counties were forced to amalgamate by the new Free State government in 1924, the Lartigue was not invited to the party and closed that year.

its heart the very nature of the relationship between Ireland and the British mainland. This new strategy was designed and initiated by the statesman Arthur Balfour.

THE NORTH-WEST OF IRELAND

THE DONEGAL RAILWAY COMPANY.

DONEGAL "THE LAND OF TYRCONNEL" BY THE DONEGAL RAILWAY Co.

LONDONDERRY

DONEGAL CASTLE

LOUGH EASKE

SLIEVE LEAGUE

BARNESMORE GAP

KILLYBEGS

ALL INFORMATION FROM MR. R.H. LIVESEY GENERAL MANAGER. STRANORLAR. Co. DONEGAL.

A colourful Donegal Railway poster published in 1899.

In the 1890s there were two reasons why Conservative politicians at Westminster were keen to subsidise the building of railways in the south and west of Ireland, in those areas which would become known as 'the congested districts'. There was a genuine desire to ease the dire poverty of many of the inhabitants, but it was also hoped that as the economic health of these districts improved the demand for a separate parliament in Dublin would be diluted. This policy came to be known as 'constructive unionism' or, in a phrase used by Gerald Balfour, who followed his brother Arthur and served as Chief Secretary for Ireland from 1895 to 1900, 'an attempt to kill Home Rule with kindness'.

The origins of government support for railway building in Ireland came in the report of a Royal Commission, led by Sir James Allport, to investigate the conduct of public works in Ireland. Allport was one of Britain's most respected and enlightened railway managers. The Commission's report, published in 1888, stopped short of advocating nationalisation, but it recognised the shortcomings of the existing methods of finance when it came to extending railways into poorer and more remote districts. The report made specific recommendations for the construction of eleven light railways, including two in County Donegal. The Light Railways (Ireland) Act of 1889, sometimes called the Balfour Act, was based on the report's recommendations. It allowed direct state aid in the form of grants, rather than loans or guarantees, in an attempt to encourage the existing railway companies to build and work light railways in unpromising parts of Ireland. The grants could apply to lines of either gauge.

The narrow gauge network in County Donegal benefited substantially from the Act. In 1892 parliament sanctioned the merger of the FVR and the WDR to form the Donegal Railway Company, and in 1893 it approved the conversion of the original Finn Valley line, from Stranorlar to Strabane, to the 3ft gauge. A new approach into Strabane by a separate bridge over the River Mourne, leading to a new narrow gauge station adjacent to the GNR one, was built, and narrow gauge trains ran into Strabane for the first time in July 1894. The Balfour Act provided funding for two extensions to the DR system, a line from Donegal Town westwards to the fishing village of Killybegs, which opened in August 1893, and a branch from Stranorlar to Glenties which opened in June 1895, bringing the route mileage of the DR up to seventy-five miles. Despite opposition from the GNR, the DR was authorised to build a narrow gauge line to Londonderry in 1896. This line, which opened in August 1900, reached the city by running on the opposite side of Lough Foyle from the Donegal shore, which was already occupied by the GNR route. The new line, via Donemana and New Buildings, ended at Derry's fourth terminus, at Victoria Road beside the city's only bridge over the Foyle. Also authorised in 1896 was an extension from Donegal Town to Ballyshannon, which opened in September 1905. Because neither the Derry or Ballyshannon lines served impoverished or congested districts, there was no financial assistance for either.

By this time the ownership of the DR had changed. In 1903 the Midland, one of England's biggest railways, bought the B&NCR, and made approaches to buy the DR. The arrival of a powerful new neighbour alarmed the GNR, who objected to the proposed purchase. Eventually the two companies bought the DR jointly. To manage their acquisition a joint committee, the County Donegal Railways Joint Committee, was set up, with three members from each company. After the CDR had been created the final part of its network was built by the nominally independent Strabane and Letterkenny Railway. The line between the two towns was authorised in 1904, financed mainly by the new joint owners, and opened in January 1909. This brought the CDR network up to a route mileage of 124 miles, making it by some distance the biggest narrow gauge railway company in the British Isles.

The final fling of railway building as a tool of constructive unionism came with the Railways (Ireland) Act of 1896. The difference between this and the Act of 1889 was that while the earlier legislation provided finance for schemes promoted by others, the 1896 Act permitted the government itself, through the Board of Works, to became a railway promoter in its own right. In the event only two lines were built under the aegis of the 1896 Act, both in north Donegal. One was the extension of the existing Lough Swilly line from Buncrana to Carndonagh, funding for which had been sought and declined under the

The remains of the railway viaduct over the Owencarrow River on the Letterkenny and Burtonport Extension Railway (Geograph).

The Armagh Disaster

Irish railways in the nineteenth century had a safety record comparable with those in the rest of the kingdom. This made the terrible events that occurred near Armagh on a June morning in 1889 all the more shocking. The investigation into the crash highlighted methods of operating railways, not just in Ireland but across the kingdom, which were inherently hazardous. The railway inspectors of the Board of Trade had been drawing attention to many of these practices for years but they had been ignored. An accident as catastrophic and avoidable as that at Armagh was almost certainly bound to have happened somewhere sooner or later. It was unfortunate for the reputation of Ireland's railways and for the company which throughout its long history was arguably the country's most progressive, that the disaster took place on the tracks of the Great Northern Railway.

The line from Armagh to Newry was a difficult one to work with steep banks in both directions. For most of the first three miles out of Armagh, trains to Newry faced a severe climb. Starting at 1 in 82, this steepened to 1 in 75 for a further two miles before the first summit on the line at a place called Dobbin's Bridge was reached. After this, it was downhill to the first station at Hamiltonsbawn, just under five miles from Armagh. On 12 June, a special train had been arranged to take a large party, consisting mostly of children who were attending Sunday schools in Armagh, to enjoy a day at the seaside at Warrenpoint. The engine driver booked to work the train, Thomas McGrath, was not very familiar with the line from Newry to Armagh, having only worked

over it before as a fireman and not as a driver. The locomotive allocated to work the special train was an 1880-built 2–4–0 tender engine which was normally employed on the Belfast to Dublin line. Whilst this had steep gradients, they were not as severe as those on the erstwhile Newry and Armagh company's route.

The empty stock for the excursion, consisting of thirteen vehicles, including two brake vans, arrived at Armagh well before the advertised departure time of 10.00am. However, the numbers booked for the excursion were such that the Armagh station master, John Foster, proposed to add two additional carriages to the train. What happened next is unclear, but it seems there was some sort of altercation between McGrath and Foster. McGrath at first refused to take the fifteen coaches on the grounds that his engine was unsuitable for such a load over this steeply graded line. This led to Foster taunting him that other drivers had taken such loads without complaint. James Elliot, a chief clerk in the General Manager's office, who was in charge of the train and was to travel on the engine, made the sensible suggestion that the excursion be assisted up the bank to Hamiltonsbawn by the engine of the scheduled 10.35am passenger train, but this offer was refused by McGrath who seemed to have been stung by Foster's remarks.

The excursion left fifteen minutes late at 10.15am. Behind the locked doors of its carriages were about 940 passengers, around 600 of whom were children. At first all went well with the engine steaming strongly, but as the incline bit it began to lose speed and eventually, at around 10.33am, it stalled about 120 yards from the summit and

safety. In a subsequent test run made under the supervision of Major General Hutchinson, the Board of Trade inspector who conducted the inquiry into the accident, the same locomotive driven by an experienced man brought a train of the same weight as the excursion to the summit without difficulty. Because the excursion was so heavily laden and passengers were being carried in the brake vans, it was suggested, but never proven, that the hand brakes might have been accidentally tampered with, inadvertently causing the train to stall.

At this point, there was an operating problem for the railway but no danger for the passengers. Then James Elliot, the man in charge of the train, intervened. The logical thing to do was to send someone down the bank to attract the attention of the driver of the following lightly loaded scheduled 10.35am passenger train which could have pushed the stalled excursion over the summit. However, Elliot suggested to the driver, who agreed though he should have known better, to divide the train, take the first section to a siding at Hamiltonsbawn and then come back for the rest.

This was an act of folly for two reasons. Firstly, it would have been impossible to complete this manoeuvre without delaying the following scheduled passenger train anyway, but mainly because the excursion was fitted throughout with Smith's simple vacuum brake. This worked in the following way. A pipe ran through the train connected to the engine which had a pump to expel the air and create a vacuum in this pipe. When the air was expelled, the brakes on the wheels of the carriages could be applied. However, the act of dividing the train meant that the vacuum brakes on the ten carriages packed with excursionists, left on an incline of 1 in 75, were rendered inoperable and were being held by only the handbrake in the rear van. In the act of setting the engine back to uncouple the first five coaches, it may have nudged the remaining carriages and set them off down the incline, slowly at first, but by the time of the impact, at a speed estimated to be over 40mph. Even if there had been no train following, a disaster was now bound to occur as the runaway carriages would certainly have derailed on the curve where the Newry line diverged from that to Portadown.

The 10.35am train left Armagh and was making good progress up the bank when Driver Murphy saw the runaway carriages hurtling towards him. He managed to stop his train, lessening the impact slightly, but could do little else as the flimsy wooden carriages disintegrated on impact. In all, seventy-eight were killed and around two hundred and fifty were injured.

Public opinion across the country was so shocked by the Armagh disaster that parliament acted with uncharacteristic speed and passed, in August of that year, the Regulation of Railways Act. This gave the Board of Trade sweeping powers to impose on railway companies operating practices which are still at the core of the safe operation of passenger trains. The Act addressed the two main areas which had been the major contributory factors to the crash.

Previous to the Act, trains were generally dispatched on the time interval principle. For example, a slow moving goods train could not be followed along the same line by a passenger train for perhaps twenty minutes, whilst a goods train might be sent out ten minutes after a faster passenger train. Using this procedure, there was no way of ensuring that the train in front was clear of a section of track before another train followed it. If the first train broke down or stalled, as happened at Armagh, it was only the eyes of the crew of the following train which could prevent a collision. In bad weather or at night, this was an inherently risky way of working a railway, yet before Armagh it was widely used. This was replaced by what was called block working. A line was divided up into sections or blocks usually defined by the location of signal boxes. Now, no train was permitted into a section or block of track until the signalman in the box in front had communicated with his colleague in the rear, to confirm the previous train was out of that section. The signalman was also instructed to observe that there was a tail lamp on the last vehicle to make sure that part of the train had not become uncoupled and left behind in the section to obstruct a following train.

The other revolution came in the way passenger trains were braked. The type of vacuum brake used at Armagh meant that once carriages were uncoupled from the engine their brakes could not work. This practice was turned on its head. Passenger trains would henceforth have to be fitted with an automatic vacuum brake which worked in exactly the opposite way to the brakes on the Armagh excursion. Using this system, the brakes were applied once air was allowed into the brake pipe to destroy the vacuum. Had this been in use at Armagh, the brakes on the ten carriages left on the incline would have been applied automatically. This also meant that if carriages became detached from a train through a failure of a coupling, the fragile rubber vacuum hoses would tear apart, air would be admitted to the pipe on the detached carriages and their brakes would be applied. This was also what happened when a passenger pulled the communication cord, though this only admitted a small amount of air to the brake pipes and the effect was much less dramatic than that usually portrayed in the cinema.

The great majority of trains today use air rather than vacuum brakes, but exactly the same principle applies. They are failsafe mechanisms – if the pipe fractures for any reason or air pressure falls, the brakes come on. The modernisation of signalling in recent decades has all but banished the traditional signal box and its semaphore signals from Ireland. However, even though the technology has changed the fundamental principles of this system are still those introduced after Armagh, with the lines divided into blocks, now protected by remotely operated colour light signals.

The events of 12 June 1889 and the sudden and violent deaths of so many children in particular, visited the greatest imaginable horror upon the people of Armagh. It is rare in history to be able to say with absolute certainty that something good came out of a catastrophe. In this instance it did.

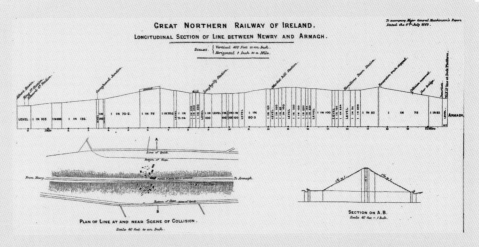

Extracts from the Board of Trade enquiry report on the Armagh disaster – the line profile and location plan (above), and the casualty list (below).

APPENDIX.

LIST OF THOSE KILLED IN ACCIDENT OR DIED SINCE.

Name.	Age.	Address.	Occupation.
Samuel M. Steele	40	Abbey Street	Clerk of Petty Sessions.
Sarah Eliza Steele	9	Do.	Children of do.
Ethel Steele	7	Do.	Do.
Mina Reilly	16	Do.	
Maria Boyd	17	Barrack Hill.	
Joseph Johnston	45	Lower English Street.	Labourer.
Agnes Hull	12	Jenney's Row.	
Betsy Devlin	20	"	Servant.
Catherine Murry	28	Lower English Street.	
Eliza Johnston	40	Banbrook Hill	Wife of Joseph Johnston, labourer.
Margaret McClure	37	Jenney's Row.	
Jane Thompson	40	English Street	Servant.
William R. W. Mullan	18	Abbey Street	Son of Reverend W. Mullan.
William Crozier	25	Market Street	Assistant in hardware shop.
Thomas Henderson	60	Barrack Street	Plumber.
Charles Neale	45	Lunatic Asylum	Gatekeeper.
Mary J. Neale	40	Do.	Wife of Charles Neale.
Eliza Neale		Do.	Daughter do.
William Walker	13	Barrack Street	
Minnie Edwards	7	Railway Street	Child of G. A. Edwards, Esq., J.P.
David Edwards	8	Do.	Do.
Catherine McCann	58	Do.	Grocer.
James Cleeland	45	Do.	Wife of James Cleeland.
Margaret Cleeland		Do.	
Robert Cleeland	7	Do.	Son of James and Margaret Cleeland.
Samuel Cleeland	10	Do.	Do.
Charles Cleeland	14	Do.	Do.
Margaret Patterson	17	Drumond.	
Margaret Stranson	11	Limenhall Street.	
Margaret Connolly	45	Manchester.	
Joseph McCann	50	Poor School Lane	Labourer.
Catherine McCann	40		Wife of Joseph McCann.
Robert Mitchell	40	Scotch Street	Hairdresser.
Mary Mitchell	35	Do.	Wife of Robert Mitchell.
William R. Mitchell	2	Do.	Son of Robert and Mary Mitchell.
William W. Holland	17½	Dobbin Street	Assistant teacher in National School.
Margaret Gibson	18	Irish Street	Milliner.
Mary Orr	15	Ballynick	Farmer's daughter.
Jane Orr	18	Do.	Do.
Minnie Murdock	16	English Street	Milliner.
Henry Jenkinson	72	Dobbin Street	Ex-warder retired on pension
Mary Jenkinson	36	Do.	Wife of Henry Jenkinson.
Mary Anderson	19	Tullyart	Farmer's daughter.
Sarah Connoll	24	Mullyloughran.	
Annie Eager	19	Ballynick	Farmer's daughter.
Margaret M'Vey	9	Edward Street.	
Ellen Watt	20	Middleton, Tullyaline.	
Mary Johnston	—	Market Street.	
Isabella M'Farland	23	Barrack Hill	Dressmaker.
Bethia M'Farland	20	Do.	Do.
John Mullaghad	50	Charter School Lane	Labourer.
Anne Bell	27	Lower English Street	Servant.
Robert John Irwin	23	Lunatic Asylum	Keeper in Lunatic Asylum.
Charles Robinson	18	Market Street	
Bertie Robinson	14	Do.	
William Boarke	18	English Street	Grocer's apprentice.
Eugenia Simpson	15	Scotch Street.	
Ernest Logue	10	Palace Row.	
Lizzie Sloan	14	Barrack Hill.	
Sarah Scott	41	Drummond	Farmer's wife.
William Parks	—	Newry Road.	
Agnes Parks	18	Mullinure	Farmer's daughter.
Robert Warnock	—	Newry Road.	
Francis Latimer	45	Lunatic Asylum	Gardener.
Mary Rountree	16	Slater's Grange	Dressmaker's apprentice.
Lizzie Rountree	18	Do.	Do.
Hettie Wolff	10	Abbey Street.	
James Orr			
Mary Jane Mason	12	Scotch Street	Daughter of James Mason, grocer.
F. W. Moore	12	Lisadian.	
Minnie Jane Quinn	18	Barrack Street	Dressmaker.
Henry Hillock	14	Palace Row.	
Maggie Mills	22	Lisadian	Farmer's daughter.
Margaret Mason	18	Scotch Street	Daughter of James Mason, grocer.
Edith C. Irwin	10½	Drumadd	Daughter of James Irwin, grocer.
Matilda Robinson	50	Drumadd	
Thomas Hill	16	Lower English Street	Clerk.
Morgh Huston	17	Ballycrummy.	
Mary Hamill	21	Lunatic Asylum	Nurse.

terms of the Balfour Act. The other was the magnificent folly that was the Letterkenny and Burtonport Extension Railway. This ran for fifty miles through mainly wild and inhospitable terrain to reach the small fishing port of Burtonport, the whole distance from the L&LSR's Graving Dock station in Derry to Burtonport being more than seventy-four miles, a journey of around five hours. The line served scarcely a sizeable village on the way, and the initial cost to the taxpayer for its construction was £300,000. These extensions brought the route mileage of the L&LSR up to ninety-nine miles, making it the second largest narrow gauge operator after the CDR.

Among the many railways built under the Balfour Act were lines from Ballina to Killala and Westport to Achill in Mayo, the Galway to Clifden line, the County Kerry branches to Kenmare and Valentia, Skibbereen to Baltimore in County Cork, and the line from Claremorris to Colloney. They were conceived as part of the plan to regenerate the areas the government defined as the congested districts, where impoverishment was defined in terms of the rateable value. In addition to building railways, the Congested Districts Board built roads, piers and bridges, and encouraged improvements in agriculture and fisheries. The Board's main achievement was assisting in the transfer of land ownership from landlords to tenants. A series of Acts from the 1880s onwards provided long-term finance enabling tenant farmers to buy their land from the landowners.

Yet despite all the Board's efforts, the population of the congested districts continued to decline, and emigration and seasonal migration to find work continued as before. Ultimately the political aspirations of constructive unionism also failed. Though it became less strident, the desire for home rule never went away, and a Home Rule Act actually received

royal assent in September 1914 (though all parties agreed that its implementation would be suspended for the duration of the war).

In addition to those lines built with support from the Grand Juries and the government at Westminster, many other destinations entered the timetables for the first time between 1880 and 1914. Of these, a number were branches of existing lines. Typical was the short branch off the B&NCR main line to Ballyclare, which opened in 1884. Also on the B&NCR system, in 1883, the Limavady branch was extended ten miles to Dungiven by the independent Limavady and Dungiven Railway. The Draperstown Railway, built to reach that small County Tyrone town with a branch off the Derry Central line at Magherafelt, had a similar history, being worked jointly to begin with and then absorbed by the B&NCR in 1895. On the GNR, a branch off the Dundalk to Clones line at Inniskeen reached Carrickmacross in 1886, and in 1896 Ardee in County Louth was linked to the main line with a branch from Dromin Junction. Another GNR branch which opened in the 1880s, built with the support of baronial guarantees, was the line from Ballyhaise on the Clones to Cavan line to Belturbet, where it was to make a junction with the Cavan and Leitrim narrow gauge line.

Elsewhere in Ulster, the Downpatrick, Killough and Ardglass Railway opened in 1892. This nine-mile-long line ran from Downpatrick to the fishing village of Ardglass, where there was a short extension from the station through the streets down to the harbour. In conjunction with this, the B&CDR built a loop line at Downpatrick, which enabled trains to run directly from Belfast to Newcastle without having to reverse at Downpatrick, which had remained a terminal station when the main line was extended to Newcastle in 1869. The final addition to the B&CDR was a line north from Newcastle to Castlewellan, where it formed an end-on junction with an extension

Burtonport on the Londonderry and Lough Swilly Railway, 1912, a painting by Norman Whitla.

of the GNR's County Down branch from Banbridge. When this line opened in March 1906, it gave the GNR access to the popular seaside resort of Newcastle.

The last lengthy broad gauge line to be built in Ireland proved to be an almost complete waste of time. The construction of the Great Northern line from Castleblayney to Keady and Armagh, which opened in 1909–10, showed just how pointless railway politics could sometimes be. It was built by the GNR purely as a measure to defend what it saw as its territory, in the face of threats on the part of the MGWR to invade it. When the Navan and Kingscourt was building its line in the 1870s, various proposals were put forward for extensions further northwards to Carrickmacross or Castleblayney. Nothing came of these, but in 1893 the Midland announced plans not just for a short extension of the Kingscourt line, but for a major trunk route from there through Armagh and Dungannon to a junction with the Belfast and Northern Counties at Cookstown. In the face of opposition from the GNR, the MGWR scheme was withdrawn. However, in 1900, an independent company backed by the MGWR, the Kingscourt, Keady and Armagh Railway, was authorised by parliament to build this line. The GNR entered into negotiations with the KK&A, and in return for them dropping the line to Kingscourt the GNR agreed to assist the scheme and work the line. Their financial involvement was initially a subscription of £50,000, though it later had to provide a further £300,000 to the company, which changed its name

A gallery of 'golden age' Irish express locomotives from contemporary issues of *The Railway Magazine*: GNR 4–4–0 No. 131 *Uranus* (November 1901); MGWR 4–4–0 No. 7 *Connemara* (September 1909); GNR 4–4–0 No. 174 *Carrantuohill* (September 1913).

to the Castleblayney, Keady and Armagh Railway. Construction of the difficult eighteen-mile-long line through hilly and boggy territory began in 1903. There were two viaducts on the line made from the new material concrete, the longest of which, Tassagh Viaduct near Keady, had eleven arches and was 570ft in length. The summit of the line at Carnagh at 613 feet, south of Keady, was the highest point on the Great Northern and the second highest reached by a broad gauge line in Ireland. The eight miles from Armagh to Keady opened in May 1909, and the remaining ten miles to Castleblayney in November 1910. The CK&A was taken over by the GNR in 1911, but the line was a commercial disaster, and was worked at a loss until 1924 when the section south of Keady was closed, partition finally

putting an end to its already very modest prospects. The GNR had paid a heavy price to keep the Midland out of its territory.

The GS&WR continued to expand its network, mainly by absorbing smaller undertakings. This was the fate of the Clara and Banagher Railway, which, with the help of a loan from the Board of Works, opened its seventeen-mile-long branch in 1884. The GS&WR entered into an agreement to work the line for ten years, after which it bought the line from the Board for a bargain price of £5,000. One branch which the GS&WR did at least partly fund was that from

The majestic Castleblayney, Keady and Armagh Railway Tassagh Viaduct today (Tourism Ireland).

Sallins to Naas and Tullow, which opened in 1886. The GS&WR financed the line as far as Baltinglass, the final ten miles to Tullow being underwritten with a baronial guarantee.

The expansion of the GS&WR also tied up loose ends left when other companies got into trouble. One such was the branch line from Maryborough to Mountmellick which opened in 1885, the only part of a planned line to Mullingar which the grandly named Waterford and Central Ireland Railway had managed to open. The GS&WR bought the W&CIR in 1900, its minimal offer of £17.50 for each £100 worth of W&CIR stock being gratefully accepted by those unfortunate enough to have invested in the W&CIR. In over forty years of independent existence the company had never managed to pay a dividend on its ordinary shares. The GS&WR also gobbled up two branches in County Cork built by local companies – the nine-mile branch from Banteer on the line from Mallow to Tralee, Kanturk and Newmarket, and the branch from Fermoy to Mitchelstown which had opened in 1891 and was taken over in 1900. The last branch line built by the GS&WR ran for six miles from Goold's Cross on the Cork main line to Cashel, terminating in the shadow of the famous Rock of Cashel with its round tower and ruins.

The existing railways in the south and west of County Cork were much extended from 1880 onwards. In 1879 the Ilen Valley Railway obtained powers to extend its existing line from Drimoleague to Bantry, but before construction began the powers were transferred to the Cork and Bandon, who at the same time took over the West Cork Railway and the Kinsale line. The new line was ready for Board of Trade inspection in June 1881, and services commenced the following month. In August 1880 the Clonakilty Extension Railway received royal assent, the culmination of several attempts to bring a railway to the town. The company was assisted

Clonakilty Junction (for the Courtmacsherry Branch) in the early 1950s.

by a £20,000 treasury loan. The nine-mile branch from Clonakilty Junction was opened in August 1886, with an intermediate station at Ballinascarthy.

In 1888 the Cork and Bandon changed its name to the Cork, Bandon and South Coast Railway, reflecting the larger area it now served, and several further additions were made to the west Cork network. The first was the Ballinascarthy and Timoleague Junction Light Railway, a 5ft 3in gauge tramway built under the terms of the Tramways Act of 1883 and underwritten by baronial guarantees, which linked with the Clonakilty line at Ballinascarthy. Work began on the six-mile-long line in 1887. In 1889 the Cork Grand Jury backed a three-mile extension to serve the fishing village of Courtmacsherry, to be promoted by a new company, the Timoleague and Courtmacsherry Extension Light Railway. The line, part of which was a roadside tramway, opened to Timoleague in 1890 and Courtmacsherry the year after.

The Balfour Act also funded two further lines in west Cork – a short extension of the Bantry line from its existing station down to the town and the harbour, and an eight-mile extension from Skibbereen to Baltimore. To promote this line another new company

Baltimore and Skibbereen stations on the CB&SCR, on postcards from the 1910s.

was set up, the Baltimore Extension Railway, almost all of the capital of £60,000 being supplied in the form of a treasury grant. The line, which was worked by the CB&SCR, opened in 1893. Almost immediately attempts were made to fund the improvement of the pier at Baltimore and extend the railway to the pier to take advantage of the fish traffic, though this was not achieved until 1917. The rails on Baltimore pier were the most southerly in the whole of Ireland. At its greatest extent the CB&SCR ran services on ninety-four route miles of track.

During the 1880s and 90s the Waterford and Limerick also extended its mileage, leaving the company the fourth largest in Ireland. The first new line was a seven-mile branch off the north Kerry route to Fenit, which opened in 1887. The main thrust of the expansion of the W&L was to the north. In 1869 the Athenry and Ennis reached Athenry, where it made a junction with the MGWR line from Dublin. North of Athenry, a line to Tuam had been open since 1860. The Athenry and Tuam had initially made an agreement with the MGWR to work the line for ten years, and soon after the agreement expired the working of the line passed to the W&L. Then, in 1890, a company with

the catchy title of the Athenry and Tuam Extension to Claremorris Light Railway Company was authorised by the Privy Council to build a seventeen-mile-long line from Tuam to Claremorris, which since 1862 had been served by trains on the line from Athlone to Castlebar and Westport. The A&TEC was offered a baronial guarantee from the Mayo Grand Jury, on condition that it arranged for the line to be worked by the W&L for a period of at least twenty years. Services did not commence until April 1894. The MGWR supported the nearby branch from Claremorris to Ballinrobe, and another not far away in County Galway, from Attymon Junction to Loughrea. Both were worked by the MGWR and built with the assistance of baronial guarantees. Another short addition to the Midland system, from Crossdoney Junction on the Cavan line to Killeshandra, was entirely funded by the MGWR and opened in June 1886.

The idea of a route north from Claremorris was first mooted in the early 1880s, and a forty-six-mile-long line from Claremorris through Swinford and

Charlestown to Collooney, where it would make a junction with the MGWR line to Sligo, was included in the Light Railways (Ireland) Act of 1889. The treasury gave the W&L a grant of nearly £150,000 to enable the line to be constructed. It was a typical light railway, constructed as cheaply as possible with sharp curves, steep gradients and many level crossings. After the Second World War it came to be graphically described by railwaymen as 'The Burma Road'. At Collooney a junction was made with the SL&NCR, which allowed through running in the direction of Enniskillen. The positioning of the existing stations meant that none of these could be used by the new line, and resulted in the W&L building its own station at Collooney, thus endowing this tiny County Sligo village with three stations served by three different companies.

The W&L now had a through line running from Waterford to Sligo, a distance of about 145 miles. From 1 January 1896 it changed its name to the Waterford, Limerick and Western, a label which reflected its far-flung interests. However, the company did not have long to enjoy this status, for in 1898 it entered into discussions with the GS&WR with a view to an amalgamation.

None of the lines we have discussed so far in this chapter were of major significance in the context of the national network. Only one project built between 1880 and 1914 was of national significance – the main line from Rosslare to Wexford and on to Mallow and Cork. This line, and the new route across the Irish Sea to which it linked, led to a flurry of activity in the south-east of the country.

With the completion of the Keady and south Wexford lines, the Irish railway network had reached its greatest extent. The system had grown from 840 miles in 1853 to 2,092 miles in 1872, 3,044 in 1894, and 3,442 in 1920. About 500 of these miles were 3ft gauge. During the 1890s, while the population of England and Scotland increased by 9.1 per cent and 4.7 per cent respectively, that of Ireland declined by 4.3 per cent, yet railway traffic, as measured by receipts, increased by 22 per cent compared with 31 per cent in England and 36 per cent in Scotland, with Irish passenger numbers increasing by 29 per cent. In England bulk loads of coal and other minerals, ideally suited for rail transport, accounted for 49 per cent of the goods traffic; in Ireland the figure was less than 2 per cent.

What sort of service did this great network of lines provide to the country at the turn of the twentieth century? Most of the canals were moribund by this time and, though there was still some commercial traffic on the Grand Canal and the Barrow Navigation, for the movement of passengers and goods over any significant distance the iron road was the only realistic option. Because of the way in which the network had developed, with one company tending to operate all services in a particular area, there was little competition. Only a handful of towns were served by more than one company – Newcastle in County Down, Cookstown, Antrim, Athlone, Cavan, Navan, Letterkenny and Enniskillen among the fortunate few. Even then the competing lines usually went in different directions. From Cavan, for example, the GNR headed north to Clones and the MGWR headed south. From Athlone it was possible to get to Dublin using the trains of two different companies, as it was to travel from Newcastle to Belfast, but even in these rare cases one company had the direct line while the other was slower and often involved changing trains.

During the early 1900s all the Irish railway companies came under critical scrutiny from their customers and local politicians. They were widely

Waterford, Limerick and Western Railway locomotives, 1899 – 4–4–0 No. 53 *Jubilee* and 0–6–0 No. 82 *Clonbrook*, a painting by Victor Welch.

MAP

OF THE

RAILWAYS OF IRELAND,

1907.

Reproduced with necessary additions and alterations, by permission, from the Official
Railway Map of Ireland published at the Railway Clearing House, London, in 1907.

Scale – Nine Statute Miles to One Inch

REFERENCE.

NOTE.—Railways constructed under Tramways
and Light Railways (Ireland) Acts
Railways under construction
Coach Routes
Joint Lines

Valentia station in 1900 (National Archives of Ireland).

perceived as being inefficient and charging much higher rates than Britain. Many wanted to see the private companies abolished and the whole national network taken into public ownership. In response to these complaints, in 1906 the government appointed a commission of enquiry. The Vice-Regal Commission on Irish Railways took evidence from 1906 to 1909, and when its findings were published in 1910 two reports were presented. A minority report supported the status quo, but the majority report favoured the creation of an Irish Railways Authority to take control of the whole network. The government did what governments do best and did nothing, so the advice of the minority was followed by default and that of the more adventurous majority was never given an opportunity.

The map from the Second Report of the Vice-Regal Commission, compiled in 1907 and published in 1910.

The later phases of government-supported railway promotion was intended to regenerate the economy in the poorer parts of the country, thinking which was enlightened, even modern. It was not unlike recent efforts made by the European Union to bring the infrastructure of outlying regions up to speed.

Two particular areas of economic activity which it was hoped would flourish with the improvement of the railway system were fishing and tourism. Officials from this era appear to have been rather obsessed with fish, and a great deal of effort was put into developing the west coast fisheries. Three Balfour routes in particular had support of fisheries at their heart – the Valentia, Connemara and Achill lines, yet Board of Trade returns from 1896 and 1899 show that their success in this regard was limited. The Valentia line conveyed by far the most fish, rising from just over

Midland Great Western Railway
D Class 2–4–0 No. 40 *Lily* at
Ballynahinch, Co. Galway, about
1902. The painting is by Sean Bolan.

1,110 tons in 1896 to just under 3,000 tons in 1899. However, there was a long-established and abundant fishery there before the arrival of the railway; indeed, in the 1840s the people of Valentia Island were spared the worst horrors on the Great Famine because of it. The figures for the other two lines, those to Clifden and Achill, are very low. Tonnages on the Connemara line amounted to 398 tons in 1896 and 861 in 1899; the comparable figures for the Achill line 143 and 281 tons, hardly enough to fill one wagon of a goods train per day.

And what of tourism? In the late nineteenth century a great deal of effort was made by Irish railway companies to promote the tourist trade. For a time the Irish companies collaborated to run an Irish Railways Tourist Office at Charing Cross in London, which sold travel tickets and made hotel reservations. The MGWR in particular made determined efforts to exploit the tourist potential of its new lines in the west. With the completion of the lines to Clifden and Achill the company built hotels close to both lines, at Recess on the line into Connemara and at Mallaranney on the Achill branch. In 1895 the company bought over fifty acres of land alongside the railway near Mallaranney on which to build a splendid new hotel, which opened its doors in the summer of 1896. Set in a picturesque location close

Two views of the Great Western Hotel at Mallaranney, taken in about 1910. The building is still a luxury hotel, now called the Mulranny Park.

to Clew Bay, it was equipped with all the modern conveniences of that era including electric lighting in all its rooms. A golf course was laid out on the adjoining land. Combined rail and hotel tickets were issued from 1898, and such was the success of

the hotel that it was extended in 1900. The railway company operated or sponsored horse-drawn cars which ran from June to September from Westport to Clifden and from Achill station to Dugort on the island. Cyclists were also encouraged to tour the area, using the hotel as their base, and special rates were available to convey cycles on trains. In 1915 the MGWR actively promoted its hotels in the hope of luring tourists whose normal holiday haunts on the continent were cut off by war.

All the main Irish railway companies ran hotels. The GNR, GS&WR, B&NCR and B&CDR all had hotels, and advertised them widely in the many railway guides which were published at that time. In 1899 the GNR bought hotels in resorts it served at Bundoran, Warrenpoint and Rostrevor, calling them Great Northern Hotels. Even when the railway to Bundoran closed in 1957, the Great Northern,

The Great Northern Hotel at Bundoran, Co. Donegal, still a favourite luxury holiday destination (Barbara Ewa Mikulska).

imperiously perched high above the beach and reached by a long drive through the surrounding golf course, seemed to feature in almost every postcard of the resort, and was still one of the most luxurious in County Donegal. Many other hotels had golf courses. In order to encourage golfers to use the facilities at its grand Slieve Donard Hotel in Newcastle, the B&CDR even ran a special train called the *Golfers' Express*.

The B&NCR exploited the potential of the scenic Antrim Coast Road by providing road trips from its hotels in Larne and Portrush, and the company even created attractions which were designed specifically to encourage people to reach them by train. When the B&NCR took over the narrow gauge Ballymena, Cushendall and Red Bay Railway in 1884, the iron ore

Late Victorian views of Glenariff, the beauty of which was enhanced by the work of the B&NCR's talented engineer, Berkeley Deane Wise.

GLENARIFF
By Norman Wilkinson, R.I.

LMS

Of all the lovely Antrim glens, Glenariff is queen. From Parkmore the stream drops by a long series of beautiful cascades, richly embowered in vivid foliage, down to the bottom of the glen, close to Cushendall on the shores of Red Bay. As the glen widens, a superb view over the Irish Sea opens out, with Kintyre, Alisa Craig and the Lowlands of Galloway standing out on the horizon. Visit Northern Ireland by the Royal Mail Routes (Heysham, Liverpool or Stranraer), thence to Glenariff by LMS rail and motor, or motor only, almost 100 miles through fresh and unspoilt countryside and along the famous Antrim Coast Road.

The MR/NCC became part of the LMS in 1923, and by the time Norman Wilkinson painted this atmospheric poster for the company in the late 1930s the narrow gauge line to Parkmore had closed. Yet Glenariff was still an important tourist attraction, and remains so today.

traffic which the line had been built to exploit was in decline, so in 1886 the new owners began passenger services on the line. They then created a tourist attraction at Glenariff, close to the Parkmore terminus. In the 1840s this scenic glen had been likened by the novelist Thackeray to a Switzerland in miniature. The B&NCR leased the glen and set their talented and inventive civil engineer, Berkeley Deane Wise, to work on it. He laid out a series of paths and bridges through the glen, snaking over its gushing streams and alongside its spectacular waterfalls. Shelters were built at strategic locations so visitors could sit and enjoy the views. In 1891 a tea room was added, and there was even a darkroom for use by intrepid photographers. In summer, horse-drawn carriages would meet the trains at Parkmore station to bring visitors to the glen – those

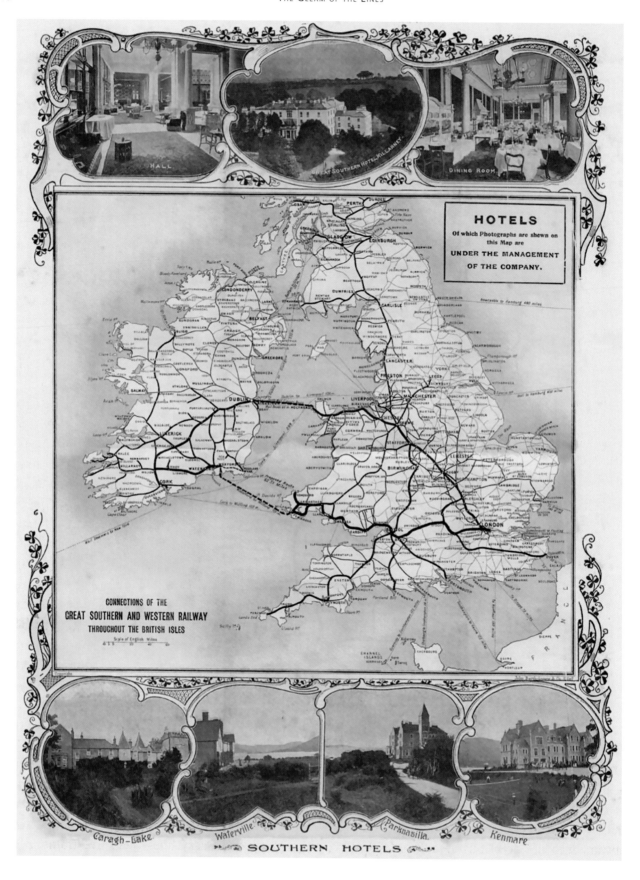

HALL

GREAT SOUTHERN HOTEL, KILLARNEY

DINING ROOM

HOTELS
Of which Photographs are shewn on this Map are
UNDER THE MANAGEMENT
OF THE COMPANY.

CONNECTIONS OF THE
GREAT SOUTHERN AND WESTERN RAILWAY
THROUGHOUT THE BRITISH ISLES
Scale of English Miles

Caragh-Lake.   Waterville.   Parknasilla.   Kenmare.

SOUTHERN HOTELS

The cover and frontispiece of the 1900 edition of *The Sunny Side of Ireland.*

Great Southern Hotel in Killarney, opened in 1854, was one of the first railway-owned hotels in the world. A subsidiary of the company opened several others in Kerry at Caragh Lake, Kenmare, Waterville and Parknasilla. In addition, the company operated more modest establishments at Limerick Junction and close to its stations in Dublin and Cork. Around the turn of the century the GS&WR published several editions of an illustrated book running to over two hundred pages called *The Sunny Side of Ireland: How To See It.* Virtually every station seemed to offer something to lure the visitor. There are pages and pages of tours that could be taken, good spots for fishing, and golf courses for every level of player.

At the network's peak there were some 1,400 railway stations throughout Ireland, and traffic had been increasing steadily throughout the second half of the nineteenth century. In 1850 the GS&WR carried 2,100 passengers per mile each year; by 1913 this had increased to 5,400. This was still very low compared with many mainland British companies, but the available traffic was very different. Ireland lacked any significant commuter traffic into its cities. At the start of the twentieth century the lines into Belfast from Carrickfergus, Bangor, Dundonald and Lisburn had some recognisable commuter services, as did the Howth branch at the southern end of the GNR main line, with two trains arriving in Amiens Street from Howth before 9.00am. The lines from Bray to both Amiens Street and Harcourt Street stations in Dublin had a similar level of service, but the MGWR and GS&WR routes into the city had nothing to offer in the way of suburban services. The line from Queenstown into Cork had commuter trains, as did the 3ft gauge Cork, Blackrock and Passage line, though local services in all three cities had stiff competition from electric trams, which provided a much more frequent service. Very few Irish lines were used to anything like their capacity. A common pattern on branch and secondary lines was three trains in each

holding rail tickets were allowed in for free, others had to pay an admission charge. Wise later built a marine version of his Glenariff 'theme park', creating a spectacular coastal path around the great basalt cliffs near the B&NCR station at Whitehead. The path, known as The Gobbins, included tunnels through the cliffs and footbridges over inlets of the sea. When it opened in 1902 it was claimed by the railway company to be one of the most popular tourist attractions in Ireland, attracting more visitors than the Giant's Causeway.

Like the B&NCR, the GS&WR was keen to exploit the potential for tourism in the great swathe of the south and west it served, and the company was an early entrant into the hotel business. The GS&WR's

The Cavan and Leitrim section of CIE was an archetypal Victorian light railway which remained 100 per cent steam-operated until the end. Here No. 3T, an engine built for the Tralee and Dingle Railway and sent north when its own line closed, is seen on the Arigna branch in March 1959, just before the line closed (Brian Hilton).

direction daily, with at least one goods train calling at all stations.

The carriage of livestock, on the other hand, was an important and regular source of traffic for the Irish railway companies. All over the country the major livestock fairs meant running special trains. The big western fairs generated much business for the MGWR – in 1891 forty-three special trains were run for the October fair at Ballinasloe. Of the 5,580 goods trains operated by the MGWR in that year, 1,723 were livestock specials serving over 1,000 fairs. The Dublin cattle market was held on a Thursday, and this involved a mid-week surge of special trains from all over the GS&WR system to the cattle sidings at Cabra, close to Dublin's Smithfield market. In Ulster, the carriage of livestock from the west of Ireland to the east coast ports was a lifeline for the SL&NCR throughout its existence. In 1914 the GNR opened a new cattle yard to handle this traffic close to the docks at Maysfield, later to be the site of Belfast Central station.

Despite the complaints made about them, the bigger companies made significant investment in their infrastructure and rolling stock to cope with the increasing levels of traffic. Many miles of single track were doubled, including most of the Midland main line from Dublin as far west as Ballinasloe, and the Sligo line as far as Longford. The B&CDR doubled its main line as far as Comber, and the Bangor branch had been doubled by the end of the century. On the GNR substantial portions of the Derry Road were doubled by 1900, including the sections from Portadown Junction to Trew and Moy, Dungannon to Donaghmore, and St Johnstown to Derry. At Belfast a goods yard and a new engine shed with an allocation of over fifty locomotives were built at Adelaide in 1907 at a cost of over £40,000, along with a third track linking the shed to the Great Victoria

Chapter 5

STRUGGLE AND DECLINE, 1914–1980

By 1914 the Irish railway network was at its most profitable and confident, and close to its maximum mileage. Motoring was still a novelty reserved for the rich or extremely enthusiastic. In 1905 only 842 cars were registered in Ireland, though by 1914 there were 10,932. Ireland was an integral part of Great Britain and the British Empire, sharing the same customs and tariff regimes, postal and phone systems. In less than a decade this comfortable and predictable world was to be turned on its head.

The railways were left largely unscathed by the events of Easter week, 1916. The worst damage was wrought on the D&SER in Dublin. Rebels occupied Grand Canal Street works for the duration of the rising. Westland Row and Harcourt Street stations were also seized. Shells fired from the British gunboat, *Helga*, moored in the Liffey, damaged the Loop Line Bridge.

In military terms the Easter Rising was a failure, but the effects of the retribution meted out by the British authorities against its leaders completely changed the political landscape.

The disused Great Northern Railway station at Inniskeen, Co. Monaghan on a 'soft' day in March 1991; many rural stations have suffered a similar fate (Felix Ormerod).

The Liffey from O'Connell Bridge photographed in 1913, with The Custom House and the Loop Line Bridge in the background.

The reality of the First World War finally hit the Irish railway companies on 1 January 1917, when they were placed under government control, three years after the rest of the kingdom. The Irish Railways Executive Committee was in charge until 1919 when the Ministry of Transport took over, government

The extension of the Cavan and Leitrim Railway branch to Arigna, which opened in 1920, took the line from the station, seen here in March 1959, to the mines at Derreenavoggy; the locomotive is a Hunslet 2–6–0T 3T (Martin Cowgill Collection).

control continuing until 1921. The government agreed to compensate the railways on the basis of their net receipts for the year 1913. However, this did not take into account the massive rise in costs which occurred during the war, when expenditure rose by 250 per cent and the wage bill by 300 per cent, while income only doubled. The government paid the Irish companies £3 million in compensation, but this was nowhere near enough to cover the arrears of maintenance that had built up. To develop Ireland's few coal mining areas the IREC financed two broad gauge branches to serve collieries at Wolfhill, near Athy, and Castlecomber, which opened just after the ending of hostilities. The long overdue extension of the C&L line from Arigna to the nearby mines, which opened in 1920, was also the result of this initiative.

The railways escaped relatively lightly during the war against British rule in Ireland, which ended with partition and the establishment of the Irish Free State and Northern Ireland. However, the Civil War which followed the signing of the treaty wrought enormous destruction on the railway infrastructure of the Free State as anti-treaty forces waged a guerrilla campaign against the newly formed government. The railways were difficult to defend. Trains were wrecked, signal boxes burnt down and bridges blown up. The single most destructive act was the demolition in 1922 of the viaduct at Mallow, which carried the Dublin to Cork line over the River Blackwater. A temporary station, Mallow South, was opened on the south side of the viaduct, to which passengers had to be taken by road until the viaduct was rebuilt in 1923. Escalating costs and the years of civil discord brought the railways of the Free State to their knees, and the new government had to act quickly to keep them afloat.

Ongoing discussions about a possible amalgamation between the GS&WR and the CB&SCR were put on hold pending a government decision on what to

The Mallow Viaduct over the River Blackwater – the original stone viaduct in 1910 (top).

The three northern arches destroyed by anti-Treaty forces on 9 August 1922, and the temporary Mallow South station in May 1923, with a Cork train about to depart (opposite).

The new steel viaduct under construction in the summer of 1923, and the brand-new GS&WR 4–6–0 No. 405 leading the presidential train over the reopened viaduct, 4 October 1923 (left).

A Cork to Tralee service heads towards Mallow over the Mallow Viaduct, May 2006 (above).

do with the railways, the options being amalgamation or nationalisation. A similar debate in Britain led in 1923 to the grouping of the railways into four large companies, and Ireland decided to follow a similar route. On 12 November 1924 the GS&WR, MGWR and CB&SCR were amalgamated, and on 1 January 1925 the D&SER and twenty-two minor lines, mostly narrow gauge, joined them to form the Great Southern Railways Company.

The GSR included only companies whose lines were wholly located within the twenty-six counties; any railway whose tracks entered Northern Ireland was excluded. The broad gauge companies affected were the GNR, the SL&NCR and the Dundalk, Newry and Greenore. One major anomaly was the CDR and the L&LSR; their lines were mainly in the Free State, but they were excluded from the new company because their tracks crossed the border. A few minor lines including the Listowel and Ballybunion, the Dublin and Lucan, and the Dublin and Blessington, were also excluded. This had the immediate effect of bringing about the closure of the Lartigue monorail in Kerry, and the Dublin and Lucan, though part of the latter was saved by the Dublin United Transport Company.

The GSR was now responsible for just over 2,000 miles of railway, serving twenty-three of the twenty-six counties. It was a private company, with shareholders, but its task was to run a network which was vital for the economic well-being of the state. Had the management of the GSR decided to close down hundreds of miles of uneconomic lines for commercial reasons, the government would have blocked the move. The GSR took over a very rundown system. The huge backlog of maintenance dating back to the war years was exacerbated by the destruction that had taken place during the civil war, and now the railways had serious competition from road transport as a flood of buses and lorries began to operate regular passenger and freight services.

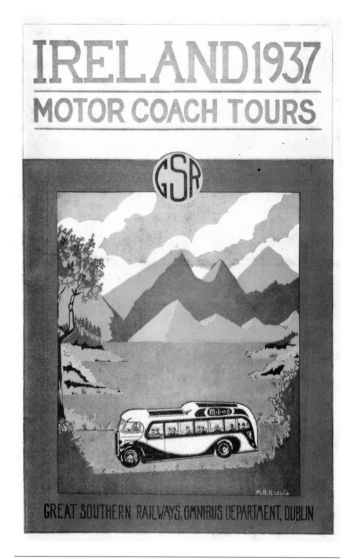

By 1937 coach tours were an important and profitable part of GSR's operations …

South of the border the biggest bus operator was the Irish Omnibus Company, founded in 1926. The Railways (Road Motors) Act of 1927 allowed the GSR to run buses, and it eventually took over the IOC in 1934. A further Act of 1932 curbed the activities of private bus operators, and in 1933 the GSR was given powers to compulsorily purchase competitors who were operating both passengers and freight services. These measures did not solve the worsening

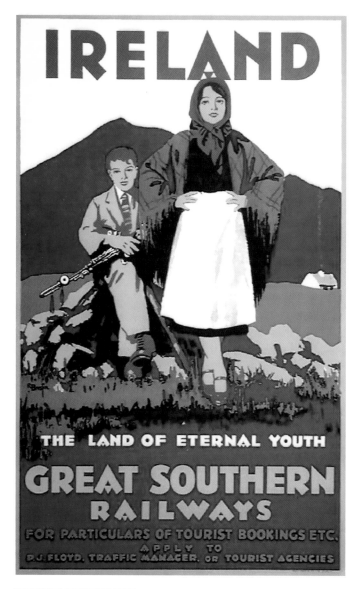

… while tourism in general was actively promoted, as in this GSR poster from the late 1930s.

pounds a year between 1925 and 1938. Between 1923 and 1938 there was a fivefold increase in the number of private cars registered in the Free State. The international trade depression which followed the Wall Street Crash of 1929 was exacerbated in Ireland by the so-called Economic War with Britain. When in 1932 Eamon De Valera's government withheld the payment of land annuities due to the British government, the British retaliated with tariffs on imports of Irish agricultural goods, which dropped in value from £35 million in 1929 to around £18 million in 1935. De Valera then imposed duties on British imports, including coal, which only added to the woes of the GSR.

The growth in road transport and the worsening economic situation led to the first major closures. The two narrow gauge lines serving Cork city were early casualties, and broad gauge lines followed. In 1931 the Kinsale branch closed completely and other lines lost their passenger services, including Bagenalstown to Palace East and the branches to Killaloe and Edenderry. The first of the Balfour lines went in 1934, that from Ballina to Killala, to be followed by those to Clifden and Achill in 1935 and 1937.

The GSR had little money available for investment. Only fifty-nine new steam locomotives were added to

Killaloe, Co. Limerick, which lost its passenger service in 1931 and closed completely in 1948.

financial position of the railways, but they prevented destructive all-out competition between road and rail. In 1929 the GSR's road fleet consisted of ninety-two passenger and parcels vehicles, and by 1934 its road transport operations were generating a profit of £80,394. By 1936 the fleet had grown to 308 buses and 647 lorries and vans.

This did not reverse the deterioration in the GSR's finances. Receipts declined by more than a million

Great Southern and Western Railway 101 class 0–6–0
No. 107 at Valentia around 1900, in a painting by Norman
Whitla. The terminus of the long branch from Farranfore,
on the Mallow to Tralee line, to Valentia, was the most
westerly station in Ireland and indeed in the whole of
Europe. The 101 class was by far the most numerous type
of steam locomotive used in Ireland. The original design
dated from the 1860s, and a few survived until the very
end of steam on CIE in 1963. The first two wagons behind
the locomotive are 'convertibles' which could be used to
convey either goods or livestock; when carrying livestock
the canvas middle section of the roof was rolled back, as
seen here, to provide ventilation for the animals.

The Irish Mail

The title of this section is deliberately ambiguous, dealing as it does with both getting the mail to Ireland and the train which took it there, which is generally recognised as being the first in the world to be dignified by a name. The *Irish Mail*, which ran for the first time on 1 August 1848, was the precursor of that great line of trains across the globe from the *Orient Express* to the *City of New Orleans* which have seized the imagination of the travelling public and added much to the romance of an already romantic and evocative form of travel.

Throughout the long and often turbulent relationship between the two islands lying off the fringe of western Europe, there was always an imperative to get mail and information across the Irish Sea as quickly as possible. The departure point of preference for mails destined for Dublin for most of the last 500 years has been Holyhead in the island of Angelsey/Ynys Mon in north Wales. In 1575 the journey from London to Holyhead was around 29 hours in summer and 41 hours in winter. Slow as this was, it was faster than coaches could manage two hundred years later. A dedicated Irish Mail coach started to run from October 1785, leaving the Swan With Two Necks in Gresham Street in London and terminating at the Eagle and Child in Holyhead. In 1819 the journey by mail coach took 36 hours.

The service gradually improved. In May 1820 steamships replaced sailing vessels on the sea crossing, and the opening of Telford's bridge over the Menai Straits in 1826 connected Anglesey to the mainland for the first time. Even so, in 1826 the average time it took to get mails from London to Dublin was about 50 hours. Matters improved in the 1830s with the opening of more stretches of Telford's great Holyhead Road, which ran from Marble Arch in London to the quayside at Holyhead. In 1832 the journey north was scheduled to take 30 hours, though only 28 hours in the other direction. When the Holyhead Road was finally fully opened in 1836, though the journey time for a mail coach was reduced by 12 hours, it still took over a day to make the journey from London to Holyhead. Ironically in 1839, just a few years after Telford's great project was completed, the previously unheard of speed offered by the new railways led to the Irish mails being transferred from Holyhead to Liverpool, which from 1838 had a rail connection to London. Using the railway and steam ships from

A Royal Mail coach in a thunderstorm, an 1834 engraving by James Pollard.

Liverpool meant that the mails could now reach Dublin in 22 hours if all went according to plan. Whilst this was quicker than Telford's road, the disadvantage of using Liverpool rather than Holyhead was the much longer sea journey.

In 1838 the Conveyance of Mails Act gave the Postmaster General the power to instruct railway companies to convey mail in any trains he stipulated and in special trains as required. These mail trains could have some accommodation for passengers but they were managed by the Postmaster General who effectively commissioned them. With their limited accommodation for passengers, this gave rise to the origin of a term often used by the railways, 'the limited mail'.

The quickest solution was to build a railway to Holyhead, combining the speed of the railways with a shorter sea crossing, so it is not surprising that an Act to enable this to happen was passed by parliament in July 1844. The Chester and Holyhead Railway was authorised to raise over £2 million to build its 85-mile long double track main line. The first sod was ceremonially cut at Conwy in March 1845, and within a year over 5,000 navvies, many of them Irish, were employed building the line. There are also a number of records of serious disturbances between the navvies and the locals in north Wales at this time. The line opened as far as Bangor on 1 May 1848 and the first running of the *Irish Mail* followed three months later. On that day the *Irish Mail* left Euston at 8.45am and was due at Bangor at 5.25pm that afternoon.

Irish Mail boats at Holyhead station in 1908.

The mails were conveyed by road to Llanfair on Angelsey. The line from there to Holyhead also opened that day, and the mails arrived at the port at 6.45pm.

The final link in the chain was Robert Stephenson's Britannia Bridge over the Menai Straits. The line through the first of the two great tubes opened on 18 March 1850, allowing trains to run through from London to Holyhead, a journey of 264 miles by rail. The mail steamers themselves had previously been operated by the Admiralty, but in 1850 the contract was put out to tender and awarded to the City of Dublin Steam Packet Company, much to the disgust of the Chester and Holyhead and their allies at Euston, who expected to get the contract after going to the trouble of building their new railway. With the mail contract came the prestigious initials RMS, standing for Royal Mail Ship, which preceded the names of the vessels themselves. The CoDSPC managed to hang on to the contract for most of the next seventy years.

Apparatus which allowed mailbags to be picked up and dropped off by the speeding train was used on the *Irish Mail* from 1854. The world's first water troughs were opened at Aber (Abergwyngregyn) between Conwy and Bangor in 1861, allowing the engine to pick up water without stopping as it sped along.

There were two serious crashes involving the *Irish Mail*. The first of these occurred at Abergele on 20 August 1868. On that day, the express passed Abergele at around 12.39pm, running under clear signals at about 40mph, five minutes or so behind schedule. Ahead of it at the next station, Llanddulas, a goods train was being shunted out of the way to clear the down line for the express. However, this was done in a singularly inept fashion. A rough contact between two sets of wagons sent those standing on the main line running away on the line on which the *Irish Mail* was approaching. There was no one in the brake van at the rear of the wagons to reapply the hand brake, which had been loosened by the impact, and the wagons ran back down the line, gathering speed. The curves and cutting on this stretch of tracks meant that the driver of the express did not see the oncoming wagons until they were 200 yards away. The impact derailed the engine of the express, but the loss of life resulting from the accident was caused when wooden barrels in two of the wagons holding about 1,700 gallons of paraffin were ignited and turned the first four carriages into a funeral pyre for the unfortunate passengers travelling in them. In all thirty-three people died in what was the worst railway accident on Britain's railways up to that time. There were some similarities between the disaster of 1868 and another crash which occurred further west at Penmaenmawr in which six people perished in August 1950, where a goods train and an express were again involved.

The history of the *Irish Mail* is a microcosm of the history of the railways in general. Sleeping cars were introduced in 1875 though restaurant cars were not in use until after 1895. From 1 April 1897, third class passengers were permitted to travel on a train hitherto the preserve of first and second class only, and the service speeded up over the years. A new contract in 1860 stipulated that the run from London was to be accomplished in 6 hours 40 minutes, with 35 minutes allowed for the

transfer of mail, followed by a sea journey of 3 hours 45 minutes. There was a penalty of £1.70 for every minute longer the journey took. By 1885 the journey time from London to Dublin had been reduced to 10 hours 20 minutes; by 1939 this was down to 9¼ hours.

Today the name of the train no longer appears in the British railway timetable, and most mail has long since left the railways of Britain to clog up its roads even more. In 2010 there is still a limited through service from Euston to Holyhead, but there is little left on the modern soulless railway to remind travellers of the great heritage of railway history associated with this route.

Let me leave the *Irish Mail* with one final quirky detail from its history, which goes back to the dawn of the railway age and beyond. For over a century, at Euston station in London, a Post Office messenger gave the guard of the down *Irish Mail* a leather case containing a watch which had been set that day at the Observatory at Greenwich exactly to correct Greenwich Mean Time. Upon arrival at Holyhead, the watch was shown to an officer on the Kingston boat, which carried the correct time on to Dublin. The watch was then returned on an up service. This practice continued up to 1939, with the *Irish Mail* still bringing the correct time up to north Wales and across the Irish Sea. This was the successor of a similar procedure dating back to the days of the mail coaches, and shows how the railways played their part in uniting the kingdom and bringing accuracy and modernity to something as basic as having all parts of the country keeping to the same time.

The *Irish Mail* at Holyhead in the 1960s, a still from a British Railways film (above).

The *Irish Mail* crossing the Menai Bridge, a 1948 poster by F.H. Glazebrook (left).

LMS/NCC W class 2–6–0 No. 92 *The Bann* crossing the Greenisland Viaduct with the *North Atlantic Express* in 1935, a painting by Norman Whitla. The poster in the inset, dating from 1938, is one of the most striking produced by Norman Wilkinson for the LMS. This showcases the new viaduct built at Bleach Green which allowed trains from York Road to run to Portrush and Londonderry without having to reverse at Greenisland.

GREENISLAND VIADUCTS
COUNTY ANTRIM, NORTHERN IRELAND
By NORMAN WILKINSON R.I.

LMS

GSR Class B1a No. 800 *Maebhdh*, built at the Inchicore Works in Dublin in 1939, and now preserved at the Ulster Folk and Transport Museum, Cultra (Brian Beck).

its fleet between 1925 and 1945, and twenty-six of these had been ordered by the MGWR before the amalgamation. It did however produce, in 1939–40, what were arguably the three finest steam locomotives ever to run in Ireland, the 800 class. Built for service on the Cork line, the trio, *Maedhbh*, *Macha* and *Tailte*, were the biggest 4–6–0s ever to run in Ireland, though fate conspired to deny them the chance to show their full prowess before the arrival of the diesels in the 1950s.

North of the border there was no change in ownership following partition, except that the former B&NCR system, owned by the Midland Railway since 1903, had passed to the London, Midland and Scottish Railway, one of the four large British companies formed by the amalgamation of 1923. The B&CDR and the Clogher Valley and Castlederg lines remained independent. None of those companies crossed the border, but for two which did, the GNR and the SL&NCR, the new political order presented major challenges. GNR tracks crossed the border in seventeen places, and accommodation had to be found for customs officials of both jurisdictions at stations close to the border. Trains were delayed as passengers and

goods were inspected by these officials, though the inconvenience for passengers was minor compared to the damage partition did to the economies of both parts of Ireland, as long-established patterns of trade, many of which the railways had been built to reflect, were disrupted.

As in the south, the railways in Northern Ireland were experiencing competition from the roads. The railway companies had been operating buses since before the war, but unregulated private operators flourished in the 1920s, and by 1927 there were around 180 of them. In 1926 the Northern Ireland parliament passed an Act to license vehicles, crews and bus routes, and in the following year several of the larger operators formed the Belfast Omnibus Company; by 1935 BOC was carrying as many passengers as the province's railways. Another Act in 1927 allowed the railway companies to operate bus services on the same terms as the private operators. The NCC took up

the challenge, rapidly building a large network of bus services. By 1934 over 500 route miles, about twice that of its railways, was being served by NCC buses. The GNR also became involved in road transport, and by the early 1930s was running over 170 buses on both sides of the border.

The railway companies also built up fleets of lorries to bring goods to and from railheads, but there were many private operators on the road, and their unrestricted activities were badly affecting the railway companies. The Northern Ireland government asked the former General Manager of the English Great Western Railway, Sir Felix Pole, to investigate these issues on its behalf. Legislation based on Pole's report led to the establishment in 1935 of the Northern Ireland Road Transport Board, set up to co-ordinate road and rail transport in the province. As the sole operator of buses and lorries it was supposed to feed traffic onto the railways; in exchange the railway

The Belfast Omnibus Company depot at Upper North Street, Belfast, photographed in July 1929 (Belfast Telegraph).

companies had to trade their vehicles for shares in the NIRTB. The NIRTB failed to deliver from the outset, instead becoming effectively a government-sponsored competitor to the railways. The GNR, though barred from running bus services in Northern Ireland, continued to expand its road transport services in the northern parts of the Free State served by its railways.

One other Irish railway company took to buses in a major way. By the late 1920s the Londonderry and Lough Swilly was in a parlous financial state, needing grants from both governments to keep its services running. Even so, by 1930 the company was close to insolvency. Then James Whyte, an accountant by training who had been with the company for many years, was made general manager. Whyte turned the fortunes of the L&LSR around, though in the

The Last Main Line

Back in the 1840s Brunel's Great Western Railway had been closely involved in schemes to establish ports in Pembrokeshire and in Wexford to grab a share of the commerce across the Irish Sea. The depression caused by the famine in Ireland and the failure of the GWR's South Wales Railway to reach Fishguard had put paid to these plans, leaving much of the Irish traffic in the hands of the London and North Western Railway and its Irish partner, the GS&WR. The GWR had to satisfy itself by offering support to the Waterford and Limerick Railway and steamer services from south Wales to Waterford.

Towards the end of the nineteenth century, GWR's interest in the south-east of Ireland revived. In 1893, an Act was obtained by the Fishguard Bay Railway and Pier Company to build a pier and a short stretch of railway at Fishguard. The GWR then built a line, from its existing route at Haverfordwest, to connect with this line. An Act of 1894 allowed the FBR&P to acquire Rosslare Pier on the Irish side and the connecting line to Wexford and change its name to the Fishguard and Rosslare Railways and Harbours Company. Finally, in 1898, the GWR entered into an agreement with the GS&WR and the F&RR&HC to establish a new short sea route between the two ports with appropriate railway links.

This was a very ambitious project. The F&RR&HC was to build a railway from Rosslare to Waterford, bridging the River Suir to link up with the existing Waterford, Dungarvan and Lismore line and its continuation, the Fermoy and Lismore. It was also authorised to buy these two companies. There was to be a cut-off line from near Fermoy to Dunkettle

on the Youghal branch, to shorten the journey to Cork, though this was dropped in 1901 and trains continued to run via Mallow. There was also a short link at the Rosslare end from Killinick Junction on the new line to Felthouse Junction, which allowed local services from Waterford to Wexford to avoid Rosslare. In conjunction with these new lines, the DW&W extended its line from New Ross to Waterford in 1904, joining the Rosslare route at Abbey Junction outside Waterford station.

Work began in 1900 on the line from Rosslare to Waterford, which was built by the Scottish firm of Robert McAlpine and Son. The route included the longest railway bridge in Ireland, over the River Barrow, near Campile. The Barrow Bridge was 2,131ft long and had thirteen fixed spans with an electrically operated opening centre span. Equally impressive was the bridge over the Suir at Waterford, 1,205ft in length, with a lifting span in its centre. Both bridges were built by the Glasgow firm of Sir William Arrol & Co. The South Wexford

The Barrow Bridge at Campile (Tourism Ireland).

line offered one of the great scenic railway journeys in Ireland with its spectacular river crossing and the line snaking along the north bank of the Suir to reach Waterford.

To cope with the additional traffic, Waterford station had to be rebuilt. When completed, it had eight platforms, the greatest number of any station in Ireland, and the main through platform, at 1,210ft in length, was the longest in the country. Waterford station is squeezed into a space between the river and Mount Misery, which towers over the site. A large amount of rock had to be blasted away to create room for the enlarged station, and the road to Kilkenny had to be rebuilt on concrete piles over the river. It is believed that this was the first extensive use of ferro-concrete in Ireland. The new line opened and steamer services began in August 1906,

with expresses from Cork running through to Rosslare to connect with the steamers.

The remains of the Suir Bridge at Waterford; when the line was closed the lifting span was removed to facilitate traffic on the river (Liam Walsh).

A steam special passing under the distinctive signal box at Waterford Station in August 2008 (C.P. Friel).

Easons

There is a long established business in Ireland which I hold in particular affection – for two reasons. Firstly, because they were mad enough to give me my first job after I left university, one which more or less pointed me in a direction which I have followed ever since and, secondly, because their history is so bound up with that of the Irish railway network.

Before the coming of the railway, newspapers were distributed mainly through the mails. However, the opportunities created by the spread of the railways created a new type of business where entrepreneurs collected papers in bulk from their publishers and distributed them around the country by train. One of the most successful of these was the firm of W.H. Smith. The motto of one of its founding fathers was, 'the mails must never beat us'.

In the 1850s, with W.H. Smith well established in Britain, the company began to expand its activities into Ireland. The first bookstalls at railway stations were opened in that decade and soon the company had contracts with leading railway companies such as the GS&WR, the Dublin and Belfast Junction Railway, and the Dublin and Wicklow.

There were three aspects to the business. The first was the distribution of newspapers in various ways, though at first the number of copies sold was not very impressive. In 1860 W.H. Smith disposed of a daily average across the vast GS&WR network of around 800 copies of the *Irish Times* and 400 of the *Freeman's*

Journal, the two leading Irish papers of the era. Another aspect of the business was bookstalls at stations all over the country, the numbers varying depending on the contracts held with the railway companies. A third long extinct but very significant source of profit was the sale of advertising on railway property, sometimes at lineside, but mostly at stations. All those lovely long-lasting enamel advertising boards beloved by collectors today generated revenue for the railways and W.H. Smith, who sold the space on which these signs were hung on their behalf. In the last decade of the nineteenth century, this was the most lucrative part of the business.

The Irish arm of W.H. Smith was run by Charles Eason. The Smith dynasty had, by the 1880s, moved on from being news vendors to Tory grandees and W.H. Smith became Chief Secretary for Ireland in 1886 in the government of the Marquis of Salisbury. It seems that Smith had little interest in Ireland, and even actively disliked the country and its people in some ways, but it has been suggested that because he had business interests there he must know something about the country and thus he got the job. Perhaps he just drew the short straw for at the time Ireland was virtually at war with itself in the wake of the failure of Gladstone's Home Rule bill in 1886, which had split his party and brought the Tories to power. Rural Ireland was also in the throes of a land war, with evictions and boycotts tearing communities apart. In the face of his political involvement in Ireland, W.H. Smith sold his Irish interests to Charles Eason, and the name of the business was changed to reflect its new ownership.

As the railway network expanded, Easons prospered. Sales of newspapers increased exponentially in the second half of the nineteenth century. News turnover rose from £8,688 in 1865 to £65,848 in 1899. Both British and Irish newspapers saw big increases in sales. In 1878,

average weekly sales of Irish papers were 99,558, but by 1888 this had increased to 148,998. The Eason bookstall was soon a familiar sight at stations all over Ireland. At their peak in 1901, Easons had ninety-five station bookstalls. There were five at stations on the two narrow gauge networks in County Donegal, and the most far-flung bookstall was that at Cahirciveen on the Valentia branch in County Kerry.

The term bookstall, which was always used to describe the station shops, was indicative that Easons also played a major part in the distribution of books throughout Ireland both as wholesalers and retailers from their origins right up to the present day. With the decline of the railways in the second half of the last century, the number of bookstalls decreased. There were only forty-three left by 1939. However, whilst continuing to be a major wholesaler of books and newspapers, Easons repositioned its retailing activities from the railway stations to the High Street. Offering much the same product mix as W.H. Smith did in Britain, selling newspapers and magazines, books and stationery, the company is to this day one of the major retailers in these fields throughout Ireland.

A typical station bookstall in an unidentified photograph of c.1910.

Myles on Track

The great man himself, in this instance apparently dealing with a road rather than a rail issue.

The railways of Ireland have not perhaps featured as prominently in the literature of the last two centuries as one might have expected. In the writings of J.M. Synge is a description of a journey on the Tralee and Dingle narrow gauge line and harrowing accounts of the scenes at some stations as emigrants begin the journey that will take them away from Ireland and their friends and family, probably for ever. As you might expect, James Joyce displays an encyclopaedic knowledge of Dublin's tramways in both *Dubliners* and *Ulysses*. However, one literary giant was, in his own words, 'a steam man', and his writings on Irish railways are as surreal as much of the rest of his work.

Brian O'Nolan was better known by the *nom de plume* Flann O'Brien, which he used for his novels, or by his other alter ego, Myles na gCopaleen, under which name his railway musings appeared in his long-running column, *Cruiskeen Lawn,* in the *Irish Times*.

Myles clearly knew his railways, but he wrote about them in a way that was unique. Steam men meet in a pub and, in hushed and concerned tones, discuss the state of the 'Gullion'. In the real world, as opposed to that inhabited by Myles's steam men, this was the Great Northern Railway's sublimely beautiful S class 4-4-0 No. 171 *Slieve Gullion*. The steam men cogitate. The 'Gullion' had blown at Donabate and again at Laytown, she arrived at Amiens Street with her tubes stuffed, the engine crippled with 'catarrh'. The previous remedies Myles has proposed are discussed. She is still getting special feed water flown in every day from Swindon (England, he helpfully adds), and the patent emulsion

he had prescribed is being applied. A sample of her condensed steam is bottled and sent to Crewe for analysis. 'Gentlemen, there is but one remedy,' Myles opines. 'She must be reboilered.' You could have heard a pin drop – at the back of the mind of all was the cold dread that the 'Gullion' would never again take to the road.

Fear not. She did. *Slieve Gullion* is thankfully still alive and well, but that is not due to the solutions discussed by Myles and the steam men but because of three young visionaries – Derek Young, Denis Grimshaw and Mike Shannon – who met in the refreshment room, then just off the main concourse, at York Road station in Belfast in June 1964. As they chatted, their thoughts turned to trying to find a way to preserve her, and this led shortly afterwards

No. 171 *Slieve Gullion* passing through Goraghwood with the down Dublin–Belfast *Enterprise*, 28 June 1952 (N. W. Sprinks).

to the formation of the Railway Preservation Society of Ireland, the salvation of No. 171, and much else besides.

Myles clearly took a fancy to the GNR, and who could blame him. One wonders what the Chairman of the company, Lord Glenavy, made of this surreal railway world which Myles created, especially as he was in receipt of virtual letters lecturing him on the benefits that would accrue if his locomotives were fitted with thermic siphons. One such missive was signed off, 'Je suis, dear Glenavy, bien cordialement, à vous, gCopaleen, Cabman's Shelter, Broadstone.' Lord Glenavy was also exhorted to support Myles's steam clinic in the North Strand near Amiens Street station. One night, when working

on the drawings for the new boiler tubes for the 'Gullion', Myles – admittedly with the aid of a glass of Pernod – inadvertently confused the straight lines of the engineering drawings with those of the music stave, and produced instead a violin sonata, inscribed, 'Slieve Gullion Boiler: Maestoso: Andante Grazioso: Presto … dedicated to Kreisler!' More than one glass of Pernod must surely have contributed to that.

During the Emergency, when coal was like gold dust in the Free State, Myles proposed the fitting of pantographs to steam locomotives and boiling their water with electricity.

Something along these lines was actually tried in Switzerland during the war. I have often wondered who thought of it first, the Swiss engineers or Myles. Some of his other inventions may well have come to him when he was composing, aided by Pernod or indigenous libations for which he had a great penchant.

One such invention was his plan to remove the danger of a rear-end collision of the sort usually caused through the incompetence of the signalman when a fast train was allowed to follow a slow one on the same track. The last vehicle on all slow trains would henceforth be a ramp on wheels, its steepness carefully calibrated so that the speed of the fast train would be dissipated by the ramp, allowing it to roll back safely onto the tracks rather than crash into the slow train.

One day Myles met John McCormack, the great Irish tenor, on the departure platform at Kingsbridge. They took a liking to each other and retired to Myles's reserved first class compartment where they whistled and hummed their way through twenty or thirty songs. This

musical soirée was interrupted only when word reached Myles that the driver was doing damage to the engine. Myles rushed down to the front of the train, opened the end door, climbed onto the tender, crawled over the coal, and knocked the offender out, thus preventing further peril to the locomotive.

Through all of these wonderfully funny and insanely surreal pieces there is a tenuous grasp on actuality with the talk of thermic siphons, feed water heaters, poppet valves and Walshaerts gear (I knew Walshaerts well – he was the best of fellows and a prince amongst steam men). One is left reflecting on whether Myles knew more than he was letting on or making out he knew more than he actually did.

Maybe it is just that if you have a passion for railways, a fondness for the drink, and happen to be one of the greatest and most inventive writers of the twentieth century, you cannot avoid producing from that heady mix the singular and extraordinary perspective on the railways of Ireland which Myles has bequeathed to us.

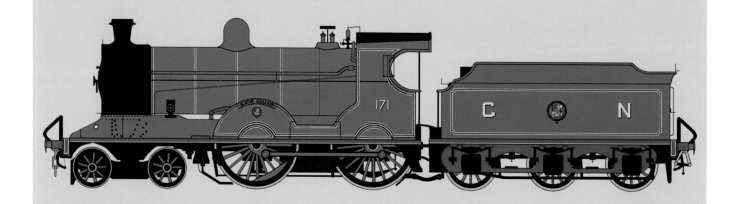

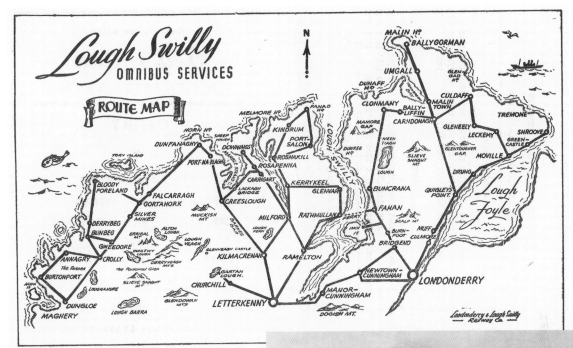

The Londonderry and Lough Swilly Railway Company bus timetable and map for 1975–6, with a photograph of Swilly busses in Market Square, Moville, in the 1950s.

process he transformed it from being the operator of the second largest narrow gauge system in Ireland into what was primarily a bus company. Starting in 1929, the L&LSR began to buy out existing operators, and by the end of 1931 it owned thirty-seven buses and two lorries. While its road services started making money the trains continued to lose it. The Carndonagh extension was closed completely on 30 November 1935 after only thirty-four years in existence. Goods trains and a limited passenger service continued to run from Derry to Buncrana, with the company's bus services carrying most of the passenger traffic, though a full passenger train service resumed in 1943 for a few years due to wartime oil shortages. Services on the Burtonport line continued until 1940,

NCC 2–6–0 No. 92 *The Bann* at York Road, Belfast, in June 1936, and a *Portrush Flyer* special, organised by the Railway Preservation Society of Ireland, leaving Portrush behind preserved GNR S class No. 171 *Slieve Gullion* (Geograph).

when the whole of the L&BER section was closed and passenger trains to Letterkenny were withdrawn. As wartime fuel shortages began to affect bus services, the line was reopened as far as Gweedore in February 1941, but this stay of execution ended in 1947 when the L&BER closed for good. The last trains ran on the Letterkenny line in July 1953 and to Buncrana the month afterwards. The company continued operating bus services for many decades after its last trains had run, the buses clearly stating that they were owned by the Londonderry and Lough Swilly Railway Company.

In Northern Ireland the interwar deterioration in the railways' financial position was broadly similar to that in the south, though the formation of the NIRTB probably made the situation worse. The NCC was shielded from the worst effects of the decline, as being part of the LMS provided significant levels of investment. Colour light signalling replaced traditional semaphores at York Road station in Belfast and in Coleraine, track improvements allowed trains to run through passing loops on single line sections at speed, and in 1933 the first of a new class of express locomotive, the W class 2–6–0, was introduced. In 1931 work began on a flying junction at Bleach Green near Whiteabbey; when it opened in 1934 the new junction and its associated lines allowed trains from Belfast to run direct to Portrush and Londonderry without reversal at Greenisland for the first time since

the line opened in 1848. This work, which included a 630ft-long viaduct to carry the double track main line over the Larne branch, cost £65,000, and was partly funded by the government as an unemployment relief scheme. The result of these improvements was that the NCC was able to offer some of the fastest schedules ever seen in Ireland in the age of steam. New rolling stock was built for the crack expresses to the north-west such as the *Portrush Flyer* and the *North Atlantic Express* hauled by the new W class locomotives, often at speeds of a mile a minute.

Like the NCC, the GNR began to struggle financially in the interwar years, but there was also substantial improvement and innovation. The last part of its network to be built, the line from Castleblayney to Keady, was the first to close, though the rest of the route from Armagh to Keady retained passenger services until 1934 and goods traffic until 1957. The viaduct over the Boyne at Drogheda was rebuilt to allow heavier and more powerful locomotives to use it, though only on a single track. In 1932 the company introduced the new V class 4–4–0s, which improved the timings of expresses between Belfast and Dublin.

NCC 2–6–0 No. 92 *Earl of Ulster*, 1936.

imported supplies, so the GSR had to use turf and duff, a substance made from slack and coal dust, to eke out its supplies. The fuel crisis extended to imports of oil, so private motoring virtually ceased and public road transport services were badly affected, forcing some traffic back onto the railways. From 1942 services on many branch lines were suspended because of lack of coal, while on other routes services were confined to two or three days a week. Main line trains were often subjected to long delays as crews struggled to make

In the 1930s the GNR began to develop railcars for use on more lightly trafficked lines, the first entering service in 1932. In 1934 the GNR introduced its first railbus, literally a road bus converted to run on rails. The operating costs of these vehicles, which the GNR also supplied to the SL&NCR, were a fraction of those of a steam locomotive, and enabled the company to maintain passenger services on many lines which might otherwise have lost them. Good management and the careful shepherding of scarce resources enabled the GNR to come through the difficult years of the 1920s and 30s almost intact.

On the eve of war in 1939 the national network still ran to just over 3,000 miles. Two very difficult decades had produced cuts of less than 10 per cent in route mileage, though the financial position of all companies, both north and south, had become increasingly difficult. The Second World War had profound effects on the railways, quite different north and south of the border. As part of the United Kingdom, Northern Ireland was in a state of war, whilst the Free State remained neutral.

Almost immediately the GSR was faced with a coal shortage. Coal for the railways had always been imported from Britain, and the British war effort left little to spare for a neutral Eire. The few active coal mines in Ireland could not make up the shortfall caused by the loss of

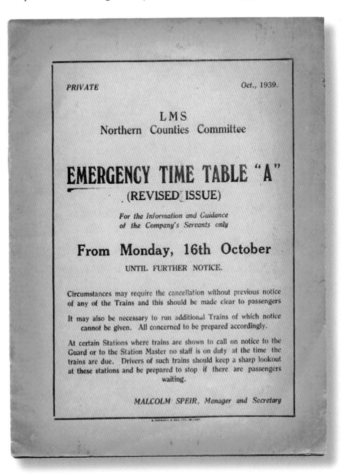

PRIVATE   Oct., 1939.

LMS
Northern Counties Committee

EMERGENCY TIME TABLE "A"
(REVISED ISSUE)

*For the Information and Guidance
of the Company's Servants only*

From Monday, 16th October
UNTIL FURTHER NOTICE.

Circumstances may require the cancellation without previous notice
of any of the Trains and this should be made clear to passengers

It may also be necessary to run additional Trains of which notice
cannot be given. All concerned to be prepared accordingly.

At certain Stations where trains are shown to call on notice to the
Guard or to the Station Master no staff is on duty at the time the
trains are due. Drivers of such trains should keep a sharp lookout
at these stations and be prepared to stop if there are passengers
waiting.

MALCOLM SPEIR, Manager and Secretary

GNR railbus No. 1, built at the GNR's Dundalk Works in 1934, is seen here still in service in June 1957 at Drogheda, operating the Oldcastle branch service (F.W. Shuttleworth).

steam from the rubbish in their bunkers and tenders. Ironically, however, the GSR's finances improved as traffic was increasingly forced to turn back to its network.

The position north of the border was completely different. Rationing of oil and petrol effectively proscribed private motoring for the duration of the conflict, but the railways, seen as vital to the war effort, were given adequate supplies of coal to maintain their services. Revenue from passenger and goods traffic on the GNR increased from £1.3 million in 1938 to £3.4 million in 1944. Goods traffic rose from three-quarters of a million tons in 1938 to 1¾ million tons in 1944. GNR shareholders even started to see dividends again.

Following the entry of America into the war, much of Northern Ireland became a vast training camp with all the additional traffic that brought, and the naval base at Derry played a vital role in the Battle of the Atlantic. The war came to Ulster with a vengeance when the Luftwaffe made two devastating attacks on Belfast in April and May 1941. The bombers were aiming for the docks and the Harland and Wolff shipyard, but on both occasions the nearby York Road station was also hit. On the night of 4–5 May much of the station, the adjacent railway hotel, and the goods shed were destroyed, as was a large amount of rolling stock. With the attacks on Belfast, many people moved out of the city bringing additional traffic, particularly to the passenger trains of the B&CDR; in turn this brought dividends to its shareholders for the first time in many years. The SL&NCR, which had depended on subsidies from the Northern Ireland government from the mid-1930s onwards, also experienced high levels of traffic; it returned to profit for a few years and started its own bus and road freight services in Eire.

The fundamental problem experienced by the GSR throughout its existence was its inability to raise capital for investment. On 1 January 1945 the Irish government, in an attempt to overcome this problem, replaced the GSR with a new company, Coras Iompair Eireann. CIE merged the GSR with the DUTC, the company which ran Dublin's trams and buses. The stock in both companies was exchanged for shares in CIE which was, for its first five years, a public company. CIE itself had a share capital of £13.5 million, but a new Transport Act allowed it a total capitalisation of £20 million, the additional stock being guaranteed by the government. The company was helped by starting to trade under benign wartime conditions, where it had virtually no competition.

CIE's honeymoon period was to be short-lived. In its first year it recorded a surplus of more than £220,000, but a deficit of nearly double that in 1946. Then in 1947 Europe experienced one of the hardest winters on record. British coal exports stopped as production was directed towards its own freezing population, and CIE found itself with a coal shortage as bad as the wartime years. Services were ruthlessly pruned back, and it was well into the summer before normal coal supplies were resumed. Some branch lines lost their passenger services for good in 1947, a year when a loss of over £900,000 was posted.

From this point on Eire's railways presented politicians with a stark dilemma. Could the value of the railway to the state be judged solely by its financial balance sheet, or was there also an economic and social dimension which had to be included in the equation? The board of CIE had very clear ideas on how to deal with the financial problems of the railways – modernisation using diesel traction and the widespread closure of lightly trafficked lines. The government's solution was to nationalise CIE, which was concluded in June 1950.

For a short time after the war the railway companies north of the border continued to enjoy a measure of prosperity. The SL&NCR ordered a new railcar and two new locomotives on the back of its wartime revenues. In a final act of generosity to its Ulster operations, and just before it was nationalised to become part of British Railways in 1948, the LMS delivered the first of a new type of large tank locomotive. The WT class was a tank engine version of the successful W class tender engines of the 1930s. Eighteen of these fine machines were built between 1946 and 1950.

The GNR used the improvement in its revenues to invest in new rolling stock, ordering fifteen steam locomotives, and a fleet of twenty railcars from the English firm AEC. Another innovation, the *Enterprise Express*, ran for the first time on 11 August 1947,

For a short time in the early 1950s the Belfast–Dublin *Enterprise* service was extended to Cork. Here CIE 4–6–0 No. 801 *Macha* has brought the CIE carriage set into GNR's Amiens Street station in Dublin; a GNR 4–4–0 will be attached at the other end to take the train on to Belfast; a painting by G.S. Cooper.

A gallery of abandoned Irish railways – the viaduct at Caherciveen (left) on the Valentia line and Adare station in Co. Limerick (above; both Shutterstock), and the end of the line at Ballyglunin, Co. Galway (opposite; Eoin Gardner). Ballyglunin is between Athenry and Tuam, and though passenger services ended in 1976, in keeping with Irish government policy the track was not lifted and is still in place.

non-stop between Belfast and Dublin with customs examinations carried out at the termini. The new service was an immediate success, and a second non-stop working was introduced in 1948. Despite the new rolling stock, the financial position of the GNR gradually worsened. Whilst income was still healthy, working expenses climbed inexorably, surpassing revenue by £118,000 in 1949. The days of the GNR as a private company were numbered, and in December 1950 its directors announced that they had reached the end of their resources, giving notice that they would be ending their railway operations the following February. The two governments jointly bought the company for £4.5 million, and from 1953 it was run

by the Great Northern Railway Board with ten directors, five from each jurisdiction, a rare example of cross-border cooperation for the time.

As revenues began to fall away and with the impending nationalisation of Britain's railways, some radical reform of Northern Ireland's railways was required. The wartime prosperity of the B&CDR was shortlived, especially as its resources were drained by compensation payments of over £70,000 in the wake of the Ballymacarrett accident of 1945, and it announced that it was planning to abandon rail services on all but the Bangor line. In response the government bought the B&CDR for £485,990, and along with the NIRTB it became part of a new body, the Ulster Transport Authority, which was established on 1 October 1948. The UTA's primary function was to coordinate road and rail services in the province, but the politicians who set it up also intended that it should not require subsidies from the public purse. With the nationalisation of Britain's railways in December 1948, the British

Transport Commission sold the NCC to the UTA for £2.6 million. The UTA took over the running of the NCC system from 1 April 1949, and proceeded to attempt the impossible task of running a co-ordinated road and rail public transport system at a profit. The only remote chance of achieving this was to cull much of the railway system it had inherited as quickly as possible, a task at which the UTA proved highly adept.

All of the former B&CDR system, with the exception of the branch to Bangor, was closed by April 1950. Next on the agenda was the former NCC section. Cookstown lost its passenger trains from York Road in 1950, though goods traffic lingered on until 1955. The same fate befell the Limavady branch, with passenger services withdrawn in 1950 and goods trains in 1955. Draperstown and Dungiven, which had not seen passenger trains since the 1930s, now lost their goods service, and the Derry Central line closed to passengers. A network which had taken decades to build was being destroyed piecemeal. But much worse was to follow.

The next target was the GNR. The closures began in 1955 in County Down, with the lines from Scarva to Banbridge and Newcastle. The following year the Banbridge to Knockmore Junction line was cut. As the UTA's losses continued, as did their favourite solution, closing down more railways. In 1956 the Ministry of Commerce in Belfast announced plans to close parts of the Irish North section of the former GNR within its jurisdiction, together with the Portadown to Tynan part of the line to Clones, 115 miles of railway in all. This not only affected the lines in Northern

What remained … the 1960 CIE map of passenger services. And even this was not the end of the closures.

Ireland – in the Republic it left the eight-mile stump of the Bundoran branch from Belleek to the terminus and the lines from Clones to Monaghan and Dundalk virtually useless. It also spelled doom for the SL&NCR, whose traffic depended on access to the GNR lines beyond Enniskillen. The UTA's unilateral decision ignored the advice of the GNRB, county councils, and business and farming organisations across the areas affected by the closures. Under the legislation which set up the GNRB all closure proposals were referred to tribunals north and south of the border, so although the northern tribunal rubber-stamped the decision, the Dublin government could have stopped the closures had there been the will to do so. They did nothing, and as a consequence the heart was ripped out of Ulster's railway network.

Other closures followed in the 1960s – the former GNR line from Portadown to Derry and the branch from Goraghwood to Newry. Even the erstwhile Belfast Central Railway was closed, leaving the sole remaining part of the B&CDR, the line to Bangor, isolated from the rest of the system. By the time they were finished, the UTA had reduced the railway network in Ulster to the lines from Belfast to Bangor, the ex-GNR main line south to the border, and the former NCC lines to Larne, Portrush and Londonderry.

Closure and retrenchment in a effort to attain the unattainable in the form of a profitable system of public transport was also the order of the day south of the border, though the application of the policy was less brutal than in the north. As the demolition trains were being prepared in the north, in the Republic yet another report was commissioned. This one, led by the distinguished economist James Beddy, was to enquire into the state of internal transport in the Republic and the role public transport should play. The analysis of the Beddy committee was fairly

This is not an overgrown boreen in the Irish countryside; it is the trackbed of the former MGWR main line between Liffey Junction and the company's Dublin terminus, the Broadstone. Services on this line were diverted to Westland Row station when the GSR closed the Broadstone in 1937 (William Murphy).

predictable. It raised the possibility of abandoning the railways altogether, or at least making drastic UTA-style cuts to the network – in the event Beddy's proposal for a core network was very similar to that which exists today. Yet another Transport Act was passed in 1958. This still recognised that CIE could be made profitable, proposing to limit the amount of state subsidy to just over £1 million a year for five years until revenues and expenditure were supposed to balance. To achieve this CIE only had one course it could follow – to close lines.

To oversee this brave new world the government appointed a new CIE chairman, Todd Andrews, previously the Managing Director of Bord Na Mona. During his time in office Andrews oversaw a major contraction of the railway network in the Irish Republic, during which not far short of 1,000 route miles were closed. These included the entire network serving west Cork, the last of CIE's narrow gauge lines, the West Clare and the Cavan and Leitrim, the Hill of Howth Tramway, and the lines from Waterford to Tramore and from New Ross to Macmine Junction. Passenger services between Limerick and Sligo ended, and the scenic branches in Kerry to Valentia and Kenmare lost their services. The closures continued after Andrews left – in 1967 the Mallow to Waterford

route and the direct line to Clonmel from Thurles were closed, for a while bringing the carnage to an end.

Given the position in which Andrews and CIE found themselves, there was little else they could do but close lines. It was hard to make a case for the retention of many of these lines, except perhaps for the Mallow to Waterford route; the demise of the Harcourt Street line was the one closure later recognised as a mistake. At least the surviving network still served most parts of the country, with only Donegal, Cavan and Monaghan losing all their railways. Unlike Northern Ireland, where trackbeds were often buried under road schemes, housing and industrial developments, making once major railway centres such as Strabane and Omagh impossible to revive, abandoned railways in the Republic were often left in place for decades. Recent campaigns in the west of Ireland, which have achieved some success in

The Hill of Howth Tramway was opened by the GNR in 1901 and closed by CIE in 1959.

Chapter 6

A BRIGHTER FUTURE

By the early 1980s the condition of the Irish railway network was at least stable. There were no more closures in the offing, though in truth there was not much more left to close. The imperative behind the closures, that the railways should make money, was no nearer to being achieved than it had been thirty years before. All that the pursuit of this chimera had achieved was a trail of destruction the length and breadth of Ireland, leaving empty trackbeds and abandoned stations as reminders of a network that had taken the best part of a century to create. This was most apparent in the north, where there were no longer any railways in Tyrone and Fermanagh and only two stations in the whole of County Armagh. With the tacit complicity of the Dublin government, collateral damage from the Stormont government's policy of line closures had ensured that Donegal, Cavan and Monaghan were also railway-free zones. This left a gaping hole in the railway map of Ireland, and a country which could no longer be said to have a truly national network. The 200 miles operated by Northern Ireland Railways in Ulster were complemented in the Republic by a system, which though it

did extend into twenty-three of the twenty-six counties, was entirely focused on Dublin. The only route which did not terminate in the capital, that from Limerick to Rosslare, had such a meagre service that it was virtually irrelevant.

In August 1980 CIE suffered its worst ever railway accident when eighteen people died in a high-speed derailment at Buttevant station in County Cork, the result of careless operating practices associated with permanent way work in the area. A set of points on the main line was being controlled manually when a Dublin to Cork express passed over them at full speed; they were wrongly set, which led to the train being violently derailed. Most of the dead and injured were in older wooden-bodied coaches which formed part of the express. Though the more modern steel-bodied carriages in the train were also derailed, they and their passengers survived relatively unscathed. One immediate consequence of the Buttevant crash was a concerted effort to withdraw remaining wooden-bodied carriages as soon as possible. This imperative was reinforced by another serious accident in August 1983 near Cherryville Junction in County Kildare, caused when the locomotive hauling a train from Tralee to Dublin ran out of fuel and stopped. A following Galway to Dublin train passed a signal at

Commuter train on the Dublin–Wicklow line at Kilcoole (Tony Brierton).

The Buttevant Disaster

By far the worst accident in the history of CIE occurred on 1 August 1980, when a morning Dublin–Cork express, travelling through Buttevant station in Co. Cork, was derailed at high speed. This was the result of careless operating practices associated with permanent way work in the area at the time. A set of points on the main line had been disconnected from the nearby signal box, and were being controlled manually. Even though there was engineering work going on round Buttevant at the time, there were no speed restrictions in force on the main line. Owing to a series of misunderstandings, the express was allowed to pass over these points at full speed, when they were set for a siding. In the violent derailment which resulted, eighteen people lost their lives, including the train's guard and a dining car assistant.

The train had twelve carriages hauled by a recently built 071 class locomotive No. 075. While most of the carriages had been built in 1960s and were of light alloy construction,

The wreckage at Buttevant station after the accident, and an aerial view, showing how the three leading timber-framed carriages bore the brunt of the impact.

the first four carriages, built between 1953 and 1964, had timber bodies. It was these four carriages which were almost completely destroyed in the accident, and in which all the fatalities occurred.

The public enquiry discovered that the primary cause of the derailment was poor safety procedures, which led to the train being diverted into a siding that was being remodelled at the time. There is no doubt, however, that if the train had been made up entirely of modern rolling stock there would have been far fewer casualties.

danger and collided with the rear of the stationary Tralee service, causing the death of seven passengers; again wooden-bodied stock was a major cause of death. From 1984 onwards the first of a new fleet of over a hundred modern carriages, based on the British Rail Mark 3 design, began to emerge from Inchicore works, allowing the remaining wooden-bodied stock to be withdrawn from service. These accidents served to highlight the endemic problem of under-investment; CIE was forever being forced to run a railway system on the cheap, a situation which would not be properly addressed for another decade.

One major investment in CIE's railways in the 1980s pointed the way forward and showed the beneficial impact that a properly funded modern railway could have. This also brought a new word into the Dublin lexicon, the DART. At this time, the Howth to Bray line was badly in need of investment. As traffic levels

and congestion in the city increased, the only suburban railway service into Dublin was being operated by re-engined C class diesels hauling sets of former CIE and GNR railcars. The overcrowded de-engined rail-cars with their orange plastic seats will not be remembered with any nostalgia by those forced to use them at that time. With locos and carriages dating back to the 1950s, breakdowns were not infrequent and the infrastructure and signalling on the route limited the number of trains which could be run. Despite this, passenger numbers increased from about 14,000 daily at the start of the 1970s to nearly 30,000 by 1980. CIE had been seeking funds to electrify the Howth to Bray corridor for years when, miraculously, during an election campaign in May 1979, the government gave its approval for the IR£46 million project.

Two DART trains meet at Pearse station (William Murphy).

Bray was the southern terminus of the DART system for over ten years until the wires were extended to Greystones in the late 1990s. Today Bray is one of the busiest of Dublin's suburban stations (William Murphy).

Two bridges, one in Dundrum in Co. Dublin (see page 69) and this one in Belfast, are named after Ireland's greatest railway contractor, William Dargan. The Dargan Bridge in Belfast, built in the 1990s, carries the Cross Harbour Link which allows trains from Londonderry and Larne to reach Belfast Central station on the Co. Down side of the River Lagan (Wilson Adams, Geograph).

Two DART trains between Tara Street and Connolly stations, June 2010. This loop line, built in 1891, was a late addition to the city's railways. It can clearly be seen how it was cut through the pre-railway buildings on Lower Gardiner Street in the foreground (2c/ Hugh Dempsey).

The Knockcroghery Derailment

Railway accidents can have a transformative effect, as we saw in the aftermath of the Armagh disaster when the Regulation of Railways Act, which quickly followed in its wake, made a major contribution to railway safety in these islands. Another Irish railway accident which had a significant impact, though in a very different direction, was the minor derailment that occurred at Knockcroghery in County Roscommon in November 1997.

In the mid-1990s, the Celtic Tiger was starting to roar and one effect of the surge in economic activity in the country was a huge rise in the number of passengers cramming onto the trains of Iarnrod Eireann. In 1998 a record number of 32 million passengers were using IE services, an increase of some 8 per cent on the previous year. However, this increase in traffic, combined with the effects of years of under-investment in the network, was forcing the railways to creak under the pressure.

On 8 November, the 8.25am train from Heuston to Westport was derailed at Curry level crossing between Knockcroghery and Roscommon. Locomotive No. 211 stayed on the track but all seven Mark III coaches in the

train were derailed. Fortunately there were no serious injuries to passengers or staff and the line was reopened by 10 November. However, it was the resultant enquiry into the causes of the accident that set the cat among the pigeons and had widespread ramifications for the railways.

Knockcroghery finally brought out into the public domain what railway staff had been aware of for a long time, that years of under-investment and increasing passenger numbers and services had reduced much of the network to a condition that brought it close to breaking point.

In June 1995, a committee of the Oireachtais, the Irish parliament, had commented, 'If Iarnrod Eireann is to continue its current operations and meet future capital investment needs, it would be necessary to provide size-able funding from public resources.' This had not happened. Between 1987 and 1993, public funding had met the railway's operational deficit but had not provided any meaningful sums for investment. What investment there was usually came from EU sources such as the IR£39 million provided for the railways in 1992/93. The Little Report, commissioned by IE following the Knockcroghery derailment and delivered in May 1998, had some stark findings. It concluded that 40–50 per cent of the tradi-tional jointed track, the sort that produces that distinctive clackety-clack as the wheels batter the joints between the rails, had reached a crit-ical state and would require major work in the next five years if speeds were to be maintained at their present levels.

Safety audits conducted by International Risk Management Services (IRMS), also in the wake of Knockcroghery, showed the poor condition of much of the network. Part of the IRMS report noted that, 'the condition of track, signalling and infrastructure is generally poor. Historically the IE network has always been a safe railway, (however, in relation to other European systems) there has been a shortfall in investment in recent years which is now impacting on safety.' In relation to best prac-tice, signalling on the IE network was found to be deficient by 34 per cent and the track by some 52 per cent. Some worst cases investigated showed an 80 per cent shortfall from best prac-tice. This report presented the country and its politicians with a stark choice – invest in the system or close much of it down.

Fortunately, good sense prevailed and the railways began to get investment at a level not seen before. Driven by the twin imperatives of ensuring a safe system and one which was able to meet the needs of a growing population and a buoyant economy, investment began to flow into schemes to improve track and signalling and to buy much needed new rolling stock. IE's own development plan for passenger serv-ices covering the years 2003 to 2012 called for investment of €3.881 billion. Whether the level of investment made in the wake of Knockcroghery can be sustained in the diffi-cult economic conditions which the second decade of the new millennium has brought, reducing the once mighty Celtic Tiger to the status of a mangy kitten, remains to be seen, but at least the work done already cannot be undone and the large amount of new rolling stock acquired will be there to serve IE for many years to come.

The Belfast Central Railway

The glamour of the railways is usually associated with the great main lines connecting the major cities. However, some of the more useful sections of the network were sometimes almost out of sight and rarely traversed by passenger trains. They provided the vital function of linking goods yards to docks or allowing through working over other parts of the network which would not have been possible without them.

One of the most useful stretches of railway in the whole of Ulster was built by a company which was a failure, both financially and because it did not achieve its major objective. The Belfast Central Railway was authorised in 1864 to build a line linking the three existing termini in the city and to build a central station to be used by the trains of other companies. Its site was to be close to High Street in the city centre. The BCR ran from a junction with the UR, just outside Great Victoria Street station, to the Albert Bridge and across the River Lagan to join the B&CDR at Ballymacarrett

Junction, a short distance out from Queen's Quay station.

Construction began in 1865, but with the economic crisis of the 1860s it took a long time to raise the capital required. Eventually, in 1878, a passenger service began from the junction with what was now the GNR to a station at Oxford Street, beside the Queen's Bridge. The line was eventually extended through a short tunnel under the western end of the bridge to reach Donegall Quay, where tenuous contact with the B&NCR was made over dockside tramways owned by Belfast Harbour Commissioners. The BCR's final flourish came in an Act of 1880, which proposed a series of 3-foot gauge steam tramways to various parts of the expanding city such as the Falls, Shankill and Ligoniel and also into east Belfast, none of which were ever built.

The new Central station with a storm brewing over Belfast, 2007 (Tim Laverty).

A train of empty stock crossing the Lagan Bridge, Belfast, 1990 (Geograph).

It was the misfortune of the BCR to commence its passenger service just as the first horse-powered street tramways were opening in the city. The company was sold to the GNR in 1885, who promptly stopped the passenger service, but for most of the next century the BCR was a vital link for goods transfers between the Belfast railways. Passenger excursions were run from the former GNR system to Bangor up to the closure of the line by the Ulster Transport Authority in 1965. By this time the Lagan Viaduct was known as the 'shaky bridge', and only the lightest ex-GNR locomotives were allowed across it.

However, that was not the end of the story, for the BCR became the first railway in Ireland to be rebuilt following its closure, a closure which had lasted for scarcely more than a decade. In 1976, Belfast at last got a central station over a hundred years after it had first been mooted by the BCR, though it may be stretching credibility to describe that draughty edifice on the banks of the River Lagan, on the site of the former Maysfield Goods Yard, a bus or taxi ride away from the city centre, as being 'central'.

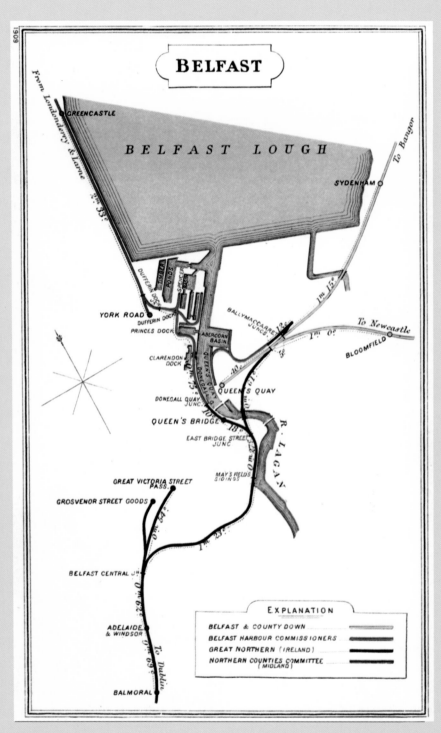

The railways of Belfast in 1920, showing the vital role played by the erstwhile Belfast Central Railway in linking the three systems which served the city.

Northern Ireland Railways General Motors No. 112 *Northern Counties* waits in Killagan Loop, returning from engineering work on the Portrush Branch, August 2010 (Gareth McLaughlin).

As well as electrification of the line, track, signalling and stations were renewed, and a new era began on 23 July 1984 when the first electric service left Pearse station for Howth. Branded 'DART' (Dublin Area Rapid Transit), the new green liveried German-built electric multiple units began to attract large numbers of passengers and showed just what a contribution the railway could make to the life of the city and the country, provided there was the will on the part of all stakeholders to make this happen.

Reorganisation was also in the air. CIE had been in existence since 1945 and many felt that the company was now too inflexible and monolithic. An independent report in 1980 had suggested that it should be divided up into smaller operating units to manage specific areas of transport, and this view was in time accepted by the government. This led to the creation of three operating companies: Bus Eireann, Dublin Bus and Iarnrod Eireann, working independently under the umbrella of CIE, now reduced to the role of a holding company. The Transport (Reorganisation of CIE) Act was duly passed with broad cross-party support, and on 2 February 1987 Iarnrod Eireann and the two bus companies came into being.

As always, the railways drew the short straw. Iarnrod Eireann's task was made more difficult by a government that was determined to reduce the subsidy to the railways. Despite the manifest success of the DART, funds for investment were cut in real terms by as much as 25 per cent at a time when the demand for passenger services and additional suburban capacity around Dublin was starting to take off. The lessons that should have been learned following the Buttevant and Cherryville Junction crashes had been quickly forgotten. The consequences of this were hidden for some years but sprang up to bite the politicians in the next decade.

North of the border, Northern Ireland Railways (NIR) struggled manfully through the 1980s, coping with sporadic terrorist attacks on its trains and infrastructure. In 1979, the company acquired two new locomotives from General Motors, identical to CIE's 071 class (a third followed in 1984), and these were used to haul refurbished second-hand ex-BR Mark 2 coaches on the 'Enterprise' service. Nine additional three-coach railcar sets, the 450 or 'Castle' class, were introduced in 1985, using reconditioned engines and traction motors donated by older withdrawn railcars. With the reopening of the Belfast Central line, two of the railways into Belfast had been linked and NIR was keen to complete the process, lobbying for

NIR General Motors No. 112 hauls a failed class 80 3-car set past Moira, September 2002 (Gareth McLaughlin).

NIR class 80 power cars: 8085 and 8094 at Ballymena, June 2003; 8092 at Portrush on an evening service, April 2002 (Gareth McLaughlin).

funds for the Cross Harbour Link, as it was called, to bring trains from Larne through to Belfast Central. In 1989, the British government agreed to fund the work, which entailed the building of a new line less than two miles long mostly on embankments and viaducts. A new station at Yorkgate, which opened in October 1992, replaced York Road as the terminus for trains from Larne. The extension of this line from Yorkgate to Lagan Junction, where it joined the former Belfast Central line just outside Central station, opened to passengers in November 1994. The 626ft-long bridge over the River Lagan was called the Dargan Bridge, an appropriate acknowledgement to the great nineteenth-century entrepreneur who made not only a major contribution to the building of Ireland's railways but to the development of the city of Belfast.

The next part of this modest railway renaissance in Northern Ireland came about in September 1995 when the name of Great Victoria Street station was once again restored to the timetables. The new Great Victoria Street station was linked to the Belfast Central route by a double track line to make an east-facing junction allowing trains to head for Bangor or Larne. A triangular junction was created when the tracks from the site of the old Central Junction to Great Victoria Street were restored. The final part of this long overdue revival in the fortunes of Northern Ireland's remaining railways came in 2001 when the section of the former NCC line to Londonderry, from Bleach Green Junction to Antrim, was reopened. This enabled Derry trains to resume their traditional route to the city and avoid the detour over the former GNR Antrim branch, which unfortunately then lost its remaining local passenger services in 2003.

NIR General Motors No. 8113 (the former No. 113) at Portrush in May 2003, hauling a set of ex-BR carriages formerly used on services from London Victoria to Gatwick Airport (Gareth McLaughlin).

2800 class Arrow railcars, built in Japan, being offloaded at North Wall Quay in 2000 (Colm Calder, IRCA).

Arrow 2603 leaves Heuston on a Kildare service, August 1994 (left); bi-cab 2751 at the rear of a Kildare service, April 1997 (right) (Colm Calder, IRCA).

2004 saw the delivery of NIR's CAF 3-car diesel sets. Here 3001 is at Londonderry on 6 July 2004 between route clearance runs. Polystyrene blocks can be seen attached to the front vehicle as an aid to prove clearance points.

NIR CAF 3013 at Lisburn, May 2005. The new CAF units have greatly improved standards of comfort for NIR passengers, and their reliability is an important bonus for the company (both photographs by Gareth McLaughlin).

In the 1990s in Northern Ireland, another change to the structure which delivered public transport was instigated. NIR, the provincial bus operator Ulsterbus and Citybus, which had taken over Belfast Corporation's Transport Department in the 1970s to run the city's bus services, were all operating subsidiaries of the Northern Ireland Transport Holding Company. Under the umbrella of the NITHC, Translink was established to integrate the activities of the three operators, Citybus (later renamed Metro), NIR and Ulsterbus, which retained their separate legal status.

In the mid-1990s, long overdue improvements were made to the Belfast to Dublin line, with 85 per cent of the £123 million cost provided by the European Union. In 1996, IE and NIR took delivery of new rolling stock for the 'Enterprise', a name which had by now become a brand for the whole cross-border service. However, the lack of investment within Northern Ireland again raised the spectre of the abandonment of yet more of the network, with talk of the lines from Ballymena to Derry and Portrush and the Larne line, beyond Whitehead, being closed. In 2001,

a campaign was launched, called 'Save Our Railways' and backed by Translink, to highlight the problems of the railways, which were due solely to lack of investment. There was no sign of any strategic vision. Funds were released in a seemingly piecemeal fashion to rebuild the Bangor line and then more cash was found to revamp part of the Larne line, but this seemed to happen at the eleventh hour, just before services were curtailed or slowed down by speed restrictions caused by the state of the track. At the present time (in 2010) the line to Londonderry north of Ballymena is peppered with speed restrictions which add to the time taken for journeys and make the railway uncompetitive with road transport.

The draft budget issued by Northern Ireland's Department of Regional Development for 2011 promised funding to commence the upgrade of the Coleraine to Derry track, but not until 2014–15. The priorities of this department clearly lie elsewhere. Despite the current difficult economic climate, it still found enough cash to build 99km of dual carriageway, including the 85km stretch of the A5 from Derry to the border at Augnacloy. The railways of Northern

Ireland, though they were provided with a fleet of modern Spanish-built railcars a few years previously, are still operating in a hand-to-mouth sort of way. While seemingly unlimited funds are found to upgrade the roads, the sad remains of Ulster's once extensive railway network are clinging on at the margins rather than being viewed as an asset worth developing.

The formation of IE had been heralded by an increase in passenger numbers between 1985 and 1987 of some 40 per cent, though much of this was due to the spectacular success of the DART. By this time the first growls were also being heard from the 'Celtic Tiger', yet when the Irish economy began to take off in the 1990s, IE was woefully ill-equipped for the increases in traffic that this would generate. Increasing traffic congestion in and around Dublin led to commuter services being introduced on the routes to Kildare and Maynooth. The latter had started sporadically as long ago as 1981, the result of another election promise, but by the early 1990s four new stations had been opened between Connolly and Maynooth and regular commuter services were in operation.

In 1994 IE took delivery of a fleet of new Japanese-built railcars which carried the 'Arrow' branding, the first new railcars acquired for service in the Republic since 1952. They allowed IE to begin a commuter service between Heuston and Kildare. Then in 1994–95, thirty-two new locomotives of the 201 class were bought from General Motors, with two additional identical machines in the same number sequence being acquired by NIR at the same time for use on the 'Enterprise' service. The new locomotives were used initially to haul expresses on the Cork and Belfast lines but gradually began to appear all over the network. More railcars followed and improving public finances and funding from the European Union added to the increased levels of investment in IE.

In 1998 a record number of 32 million passengers used IE services, an increase of some 8 per cent on the previous year. However, the economic leap forward, increased passenger numbers and longer commuter journeys from places like Drogheda and Longford, in part a response to rocketing house prices in Dublin, were stretching the capacity of the railways almost to breaking point as a result of the legacy of the cuts in investment levels which dated back to the 1980s. A relatively minor derailment in 1997 set off a reaction which could have had disastrous consequences for the railways of the Republic of Ireland but which, with the benefit of hindsight, was the catalyst for a complete change in the attitude of the Irish state towards its railways.

The Knockcroghery derailment and the critical reports that came in its wake highlighted how much of the IR network was overstretched and underfunded. The railways had once again reached another Rubicon where stark choices had to be confronted: investment or yet further retrenchment. Fortunately and wisely, the politicians chose investment, which began to flow into the railways at levels never hitherto seen. In the space of less than a decade, huge changes had taken place. The railways of the Republic, after years of decline, were at last moving forward again. Scores of new railcars were delivered, allowing older rolling stock to be withdrawn. The first new city centre station to be built in Dublin for over a hundred years opened at Spencer Dock in 2007. The old MGWR line to Maynooth has been doubled and part of the former Dublin and Meath line from Clonsilla to Dunboyne was rebuilt and reopened for passenger trains in 2010. The last passenger train had called at Dunboyne in

An Irish Rail InterCity service from Sligo to Dublin approaches Jackson's Bridge on a snowy winter's evening in January 2010. The train is made up of a single class 22000 six-car railcar set numbered 22241 (Bart Busschots).

The Dublin–Belfast *Enterprise Express* is an important high-speed link between the island's two largest cities – run jointly by NI Railways and Iarnrod Eireann, it offers eight journeys in each direction every weekday and five on Sundays (Cian Ginty, top; Matt Thorpe, bottom).

1947. New and long-closed stations have been opened and the abandoned line from Cork to Midleton has also been reopened. Passenger services have been restored to the Limerick to Galway line north of Ennis for the first time since 1976. There are plans to quadruple and electrify the tracks leading to Heuston station in Dublin and to connect these to the rest of the DART system. Many miles of track have been replaced, as has most of the old mechanical signalling system as CTC has spread across the country.

The one downside to all of this is the catastrophic decline in IE's freight traffic. In part this is due to the loss of some traditional freight traffic as the industries they served, such as the production of sugar from sugar beet and the Irish fertiliser industry, have closed down. Other freight is now transported by road because hauliers have undercut the railways. Politicians provide subsidies and investment for passenger services but do not extend this logic to encouraging rail freight to survive, let alone grow. As heavy lorries belching out diesel fumes continue to congest and pollute towns and cities throughout Ireland, why are the railways not being officially encouraged to provide some sort of alternative to the road hauliers?

The railways of Ireland have had a chequered career since the first train ran from Dublin to Kingstown in 1834. From that modest beginning, the railways spread out throughout the nineteenth century to reach into every part of the island. Changing economic and political circumstances in the last century plunged them into a period of decline and uncertainty which lasted from the 1920s through to the 1980s. Some questioned whether railways had any long-term future in the country, yet now into their third century, at least in the Republic, this question is no longer asked. It is doubtful, given the state of the Irish economy

in the wake of the monumental economic crisis the Republic has had to face at the start of the second decade of the new millennium, whether the levels of investment seen in recent times can be sustained. However, what has already been achieved cannot be taken away – though one unwelcome echo of the past occurred in 2010 with the ending of the pathetically inadequate passenger service on the last remaining section of Ireland's last main line between Rosslare and Wexford. Let us hope that this is no more than a blip, a temporary aberration, and not typical of what to expect in the future.

South of the border the future of the railways now looks brighter than it has done for the last fifty years. Some railway romantics may regret the eclipse of trains of locomotive-hauled coaches by the ubiquitous railcars. They will look back with nostalgia to the era of semaphore signals and the signal boxes from which they were operated, now replaced by coloured lights operated from distant control rooms. Perhaps they fondly remember the comforting clickety clack of wheels on rail joints, which has now been replaced by many miles of smooth continuously welded track. However, for the vast majority of passengers, it is the speed, frequency and reliability of the service that is paramount, and these advantages of the modern railway have led to the increase in passenger numbers.

Railways have always been in a state of development and evolution. The lines still open now offer faster and more frequent services than they ever did in the past. In the nineteenth century, when the railways were spreading across the country, they represented the spirit of the age. They were the very embodiment of the self confidence of the Victorian age, seen as the tangible driving force for the ideas of progress and improvement which motivated so many in that era. In the twenty-first century, the railways can again be cast in the vanguard of a different set of values, matching in importance and intensity those of their

The first of the next batch of new railcars for NIR, the class 4000, arrives at Belfast Docks, March 2011 (Translink NIR).

nineteenth-century progenitors, though this time in a very different direction.

The railway is the most efficient and environmentally friendly form of land transport. With the future of the planet an ever increasing concern, further development and investment in the railways can make a very real contribution to cutting down on the damage that the industrial age, which ironically the railways played such a large part in creating, has inflicted on the environment. There is also the sheer pleasure that a railway journey can give. It is still the most civilised form of transport and often more than just a means of getting from place to place. There is much to enjoy from the window of a train as it smoothly takes us through the landscape, especially on some of the more spectacular and scenic stretches of the lines which are still in business. On fine summer days the gleam of the lines, that unique intensity of brightness created when steel rails are polished by steel wheels, will continue to shine for a long time to come, as useful and as relevant as when they were first laid down.

ATLAS SECTION

The Railway Clearing House was set up by a number of British railway companies in the 1840s to apportion traffic receipts that came from journeys which took a passenger or a consignment of goods over the tracks of more than one company. The organisation was given formal status in an act of parliament passed in 1850. It was involved in an variety of activities over the years, including recommending the use of Greenwich Mean Time as the standard measurement of time to be used by all railway companies, and developing improved types of wagons which could run on the lines of all the participating companies.

As part of its key function, sharing revenues fairly between the railway companies, the RCH produced a series of maps. Whilst eminently practical, these were also beautifully produced, and distinguished the lines of the different companies in an array of colours. The RCH map of Ireland reproduced in the final pages of this book shows the Irish railway network close to its greatest extent, in around 1907. The map can be dated as it shows the ill-starred and short-lived Castleblayney to Armagh line as under construction, while the slightly later Strabane and Letterkenny Railway, which opened in January 1909, does not feature. In addition to the railway network, the map also shows the huge variety of steamer services which operated on the Irish Sea at this time, and the road services, still predominantly horse-powered and not as yet a serious challenge to the railways, which were available to the Edwardian traveller. This is a fascinating window to a world – long gone – when the railways offered a service to virtually every part of Ireland.

IRELAND

REVISED BY THE VARIOUS COMPANIES.

Natural Scale   1 : 575,000

English Miles.

10   5   0   10   20   30

Irish Miles.

10   5   0   5   10   15   20

EXPLANATION.

Ballycastle	Dundalk, Newry & Greenore (L. & N.-W.)
Belfast & County Down	Great Northern
Belfast & Northern Counties (Midland Railway)	Great Southern & Western
Cavan & Leitrim	Londonderry & Lough Swilly
Clogher Valley	Midland Great Western
Cork, Bandon & South Coast	Schull & Skibbereen
Cork, Blackrock & Passage	Sligo, Leitrim & Northern Counties
Cork & Macroom Direct	Timoleague & Courtmacsherry
Cork & Muskerry	Tralee & Dingle
Dublin & South-Eastern	Waterford & Tramore
	West Clare

Canals	————
Coach and Car Routes	·······
Motor Road Routes	+++++
Steamer Routes	--------
Railways in progress	- - - - -
Halts (Platforms)	*Hilden*

55

N

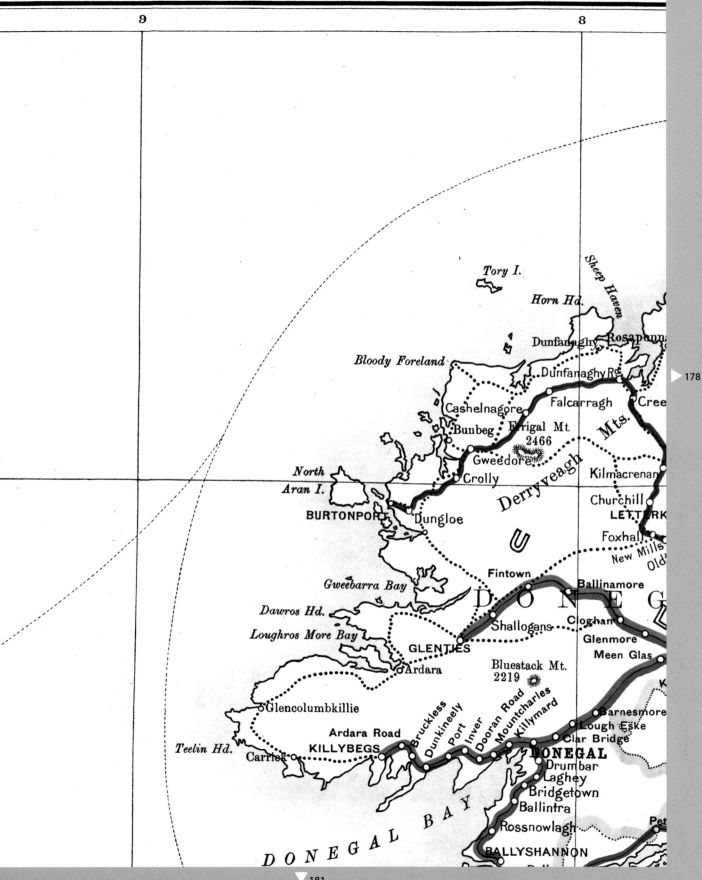

▶ 178

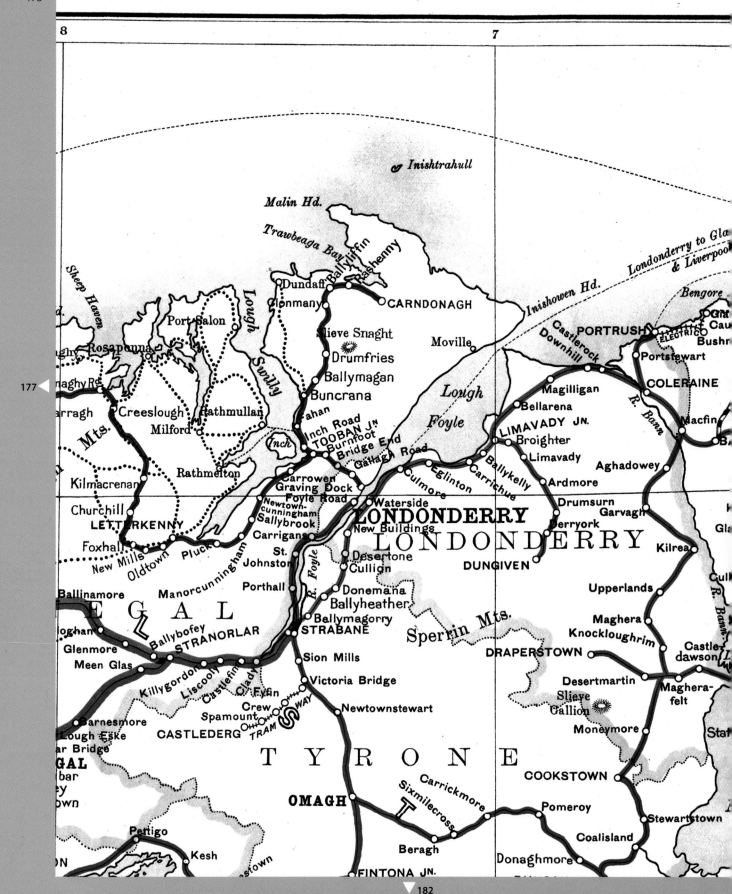

Inishtrahull

Malin Hd.

Trawbeaga Bay

Ballyliffin
Rashenny
Dundaff
Clonmany
CARNDONAGH

Sheep Haven

Port Salon

Lough Swilly

Rosapenna

Slieve Snaght
Drumfries
Ballymagan
Buncrana

Moville

Lough Foyle

Londonderry to Gla & Liverpool

Inishowen Hd.

Castlerock
Downhill
PORTRUSH

Bengore

ELECTRIC
Bushn

Portstewart

COLERAINE

Magilligan
Bellarena

R. Bann

Macfin

Creeslough
Milford
Rathmullan

Fahan
Inch Road
TOOBAN JN.
Burnfoot
Bridge End
Gallagh Road

LIMAVADY JN.
Broighter
Limavady

Aghadowey
Ardmore

Kilmacrenan

Rathmelton

Inch

Carrowen
Graving Dock
Foyle Road
Newtown-
cunningham
Sallybrook
Carrigans

Culmore
Eglinton
Carrichue
Ballykelly

Churchill
LETTERKENNY

Foxhall
New Mills
Oldtown
Pluck

St.
Johnston

Waterside
LONDONDERRY
New Buildings

LONDONDERRY

Drumsurn
Garvagh
Derryork

Gla

Kilrea

R. Foyle

Desertone
Cullion

DUNGIVEN

Manorcunningham
Porthall

Donemana
Ballyheather
Ballymagorry
STRABANE

Sperrin Mts.

Upperlands

Maghera
Knockloughrim

Castle-
dawson

DRAPERSTOWN

Ballybofey
STRANORLAR

Sion Mills

Desertmartin
Slieve
Gallion

Maghera-
felt

Glenmore
Meen Glas

Killygordon
Liscooly
Castlefin
Clady
Fyfin
Crew
Spamount
TRAM WAY
CASTLEDERG

Victoria Bridge

Newtownstewart

Moneymore

Sta

Barnesmore
Lough Eske
r Bridge

GAL
bar
ey
own

Pettigo

Kesh

CASTLEDERG

T Y R O N E

Carrickmore
Sixmilecross

OMAGH

COOKSTOWN

Pomeroy
Coalisland

Stewartstown

Beragh

Donaghmore

FINTONA JN.

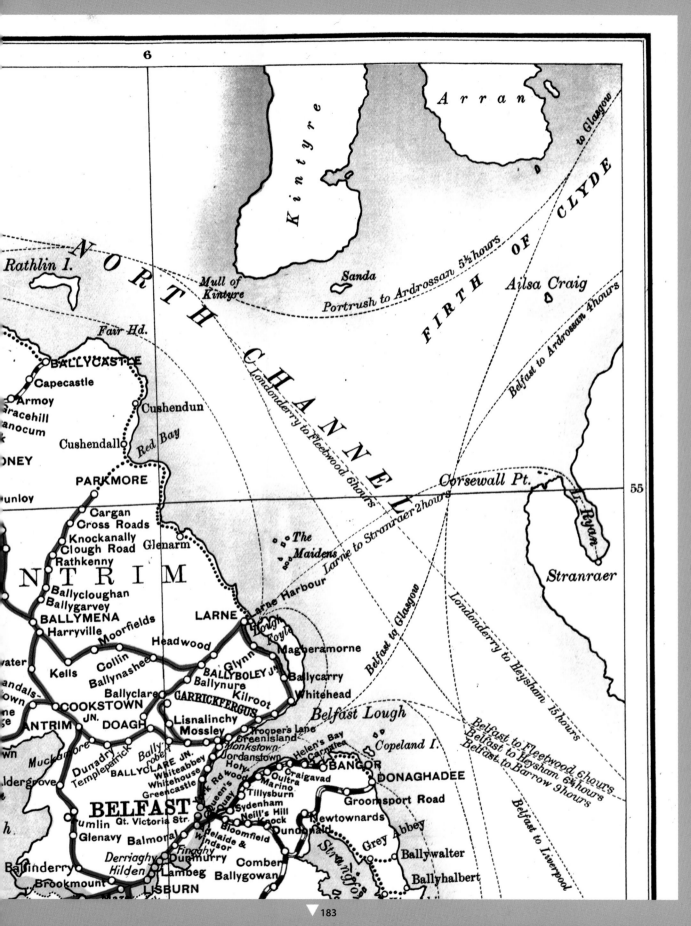

6

Rathlin I.

A r r a n

to Glasgow

Mull of Kintyre

Sanda

K
i
n
t
y
r
e

N O R T H

Portrush to Ardrossan 5½ hours

FIRTH OF CLYDE

Ailsa Craig

Fair Hd.

Belfast to Ardrossan 4hours

BALLYCASTLE

Capecastle

Armoy

Cushendun

racehill

C H A N N E L

anocum

Cushendall

Red Bay

ONEY

Londonderry to Fleetwood 6hours

PARKMORE

unloy

Corsewall Pt.

L. Ryan

55

Cargan
Cross Roads

The

Larne to Stranraer 2hours

Knockanally
Clough Road   Glenarm

Maidens

Rathkenny

Stranraer

N T R I M

Ballycloughan

Larne Harbour

Belfast to Glasgow

Ballygarvey

LARNE

Londonderry to Heysham 15hours

BALLYMENA

Moorfields

Lough

Harryville

Headwood

Larne

Magheramorne

water

Collin

Glynn

Kells   Ballynashee

BALLYBOLEY J?

Ballycarry

ndals-

Ballynure

Whitehead

own

Ballyclare   Kilroot

ne

COOKSTOWN   CARRICKFERGUS

Belfast Lough

JN.

Lisnalinchy

ANTRIM   DOAGH

Mossley

Belfast to Fleetwood 6hours

own

Trooper's Lane

Belfast to Heysham 6¾ hours

Ball

Greenisland

Helen's Bay

Copeland I.

Belfast to Barrow 9hours

Dunadry   robert

Monkstown

Carngea

Muck more

Templepatrick   BALLYCLARE JN.

Jordanstown

BANGOR

DONAGHADEE

ldergrove

Whiteabbey

Holy

Craigavad

Whitehouse

k Rd wood

Oultra

Groomsport Road

Greencastle

Marino

Queen's

Tillysburn

BELFAST

Quay

Sydenham

Newtownards

umlin   Gt. Victoria Str.

Neill's Hill

Knock

Glenavy   Balmoral

Bloomfield

Dundonald

Grey Abbey

h

Adelaide &

Windsor

Ballywalter

Derriaghy   Finaghy

Comber

Belfast to Liverpool

Ballinderry   Hilden   Dunmurry

Ballygowan

Ballyhalbert

Brookmount   Lambeg

Strangf

LISBURN

A

C

E

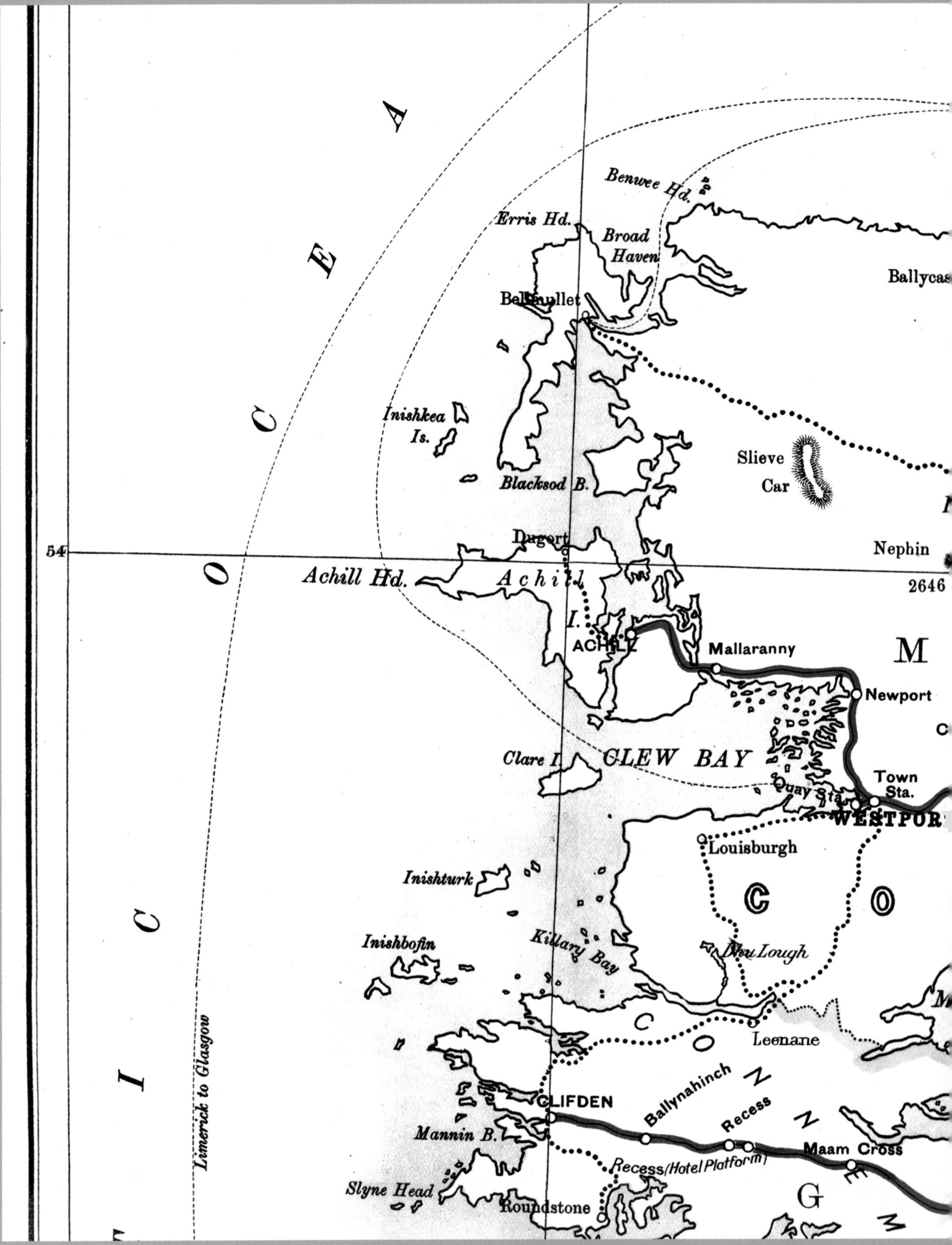

O

C

I

C

Limerick to Glasgow

Benwee Hd.

Erris Hd.

Broad Haven

Ballycas

Ball
ullet

Inishkea
Is.

Blacksod B.

Slieve
Car

Nephin

54

Dugort

Achill Hd.

Achill

I.

ACHILL

Mallaranny

M

Newport

C

Clare I.

GLEW BAY

Town
Sta.

Quay Sta.

WESTPOR

Louisburgh

C

O

Inishturk

Inishbofin

Killary Bay

Deu Lough

Leenane

M

C

O

CLIFDEN

Ballynahinch

Recess

N

N

Mannin B.

Recess (Hotel Platform)

Maam Cross

E

Slyne Head

Roundstone

G

M

2646

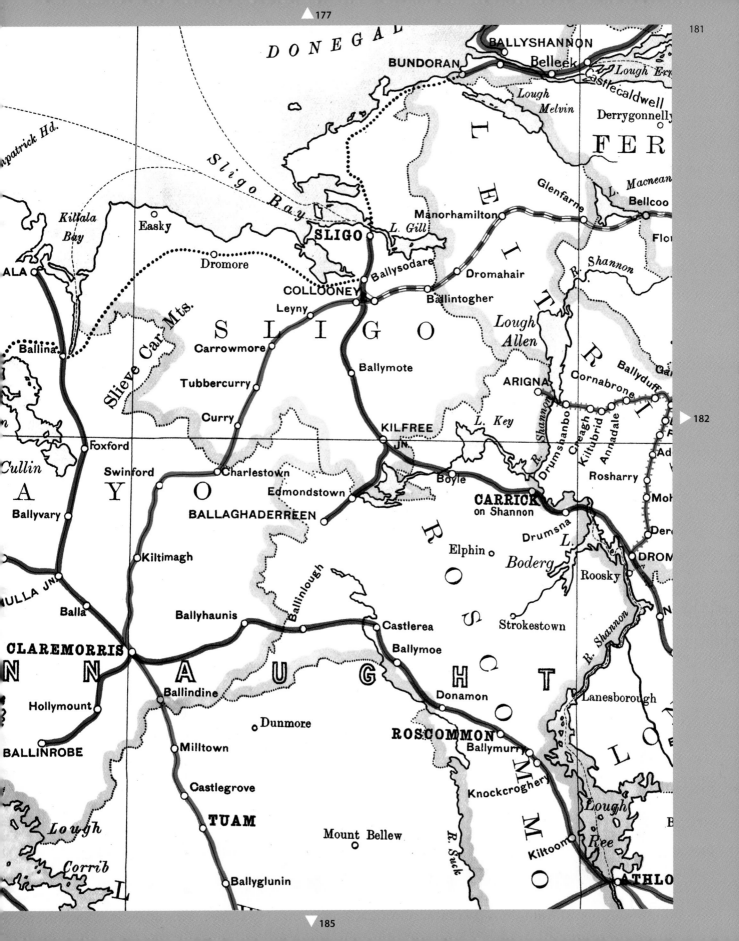

FERMANAGH

Kesh
Irvinestown
Beragh
FINTONA JN.
FINTONA
Donaghmore
DUNGANNON
Trew & Moy
Vernersbridge
Annaghmore
PORTADOW

Dromore Road
Ballygawley
Aughnacloy
Richhill
Trillick
BUNDORAN JN.
Augher
Clogher
Caledon
Killylea
Tande
Ham
Ballinamallard
Castlecaldwell
Lough Erne
Derrygonnelly
ENNISKILLEN
Fivemiletown
Colebrooke
TYNAN
Tynan
& Caledon
ARMAGH
Markethill
Ba

L. Macnean
Lisbellaw
Brookeborough
Blackwater
ARMAG
Loughgi

Bellcoo
MAGUIRESBRIDGE
Lisnaskea
MONAGHAN
Florencecourt
Shannon
CANAL
Smithborough
Newtownbutler
ULSTER
Newbliss
Monaghan Road
Ballybay
Castleblayney

Upper
Lough
Erne
Ballyconnell
CLONES
Rockcorry
Ballyheady
BELTURBET
Bawnboy Road
& Templeport
Killyran
Redhills
CANAL
Ballyhaise
COOTEHILL
Culloville
Garadice
Lough
Oughter
Essexfo
Iniske

Ballyduff
Ballinamore
KILLESHANDRA
CAVAN
CARRICKMACROSS
DUN

Kilnabron
Annadale
Lawderdale
Fenagh
Arva Road
Crossdoney
KINGSCOURT
Castlebellin

Adoon
ARDEE
Rosharry
Drumhawnagh
Kilmainham
Wood

Mohill
Lough
Sheelin
Nobber
Co

Dereen
L.
Gowna
Ballywillan
OLDCASTLE
DROMOD
Roosky
Newtownforbes
Virginia
Road
Wilkinstown

R. Shannon
LONGFORD
Float
Castlepollard
Kells
Ballybeg
Gibbstown

Lanesborough
Edgeworthstown
Street
& Rathowen
L. Derravaragh
ATHBOY
NAVAN
MEAT

Ballynacargy
INNY JN.
Multyfarnham
Clonhugh
Bective
Lough
Ree
ROYAL CANAL
L. Owel
Trim
Kilmessan
Ballymahon
WEST
MEATH
R. Boyne

Ballymore
MULLINGAR
Dru
ATHLONE
Castletown
Killucan
L. Ennel
Hill of Down
Moyvalley
Enfield
ROYAL
Lerns Lock
Kilcock
Leigh
Streamstown